HIGH RELIEF

Aphrodite I. Carving in English alabaster; life size

HIGH RELIEF

The Autobiography of

SIR CHARLES WHEELER

SCULPTOR

COUNTRY LIFE BOOKS

First published in 1968 for
Country Life Books
By The Hamlyn Publishing Group Ltd.
Hamlyn House, Feltham, Middlesex
Printed in Great Britain by
Robert MacLehose and Co. Ltd
The University Press, Glasgow

CONTENTS

ILLUSTRATIONS

ILLUSTRATIONS

INTRODUCTION

TO SHARPEN A CHISEL, not to cut a quill, that is my business. If I do the former badly I must be blamed; if I do the latter ill I hope I shall be more readily forgiven. Perhaps I should give my main excuse for having agreed to write my life at all. It is this, that having practised sculpture for more than fifty years, during a half century which history will record as one of unprecedented change, in the art-world no less than in the world in general, I have been able to look about me to see what has been going on from points of vantage.

Year has followed year of exciting happenings from my earliest day to this, and comment upon them from one who has sculpted in them without ceasing, and who has held the high office of President of the Royal Academy for a decade, may not be without some value when a calmer assessment of their distortions is made.

It is inevitable that as my story is being set down my views will find their way in. I lay no claim, of course, to their infallibility — it would be a brave and foolish person who did — but whatever they may be they will not draw any of their validity — if they have any at all — from the expressed opinion of others. Indeed they will often be found to be quite opposed to prevailing persuasions. However, it is not uncommon for the unpopular view to contain a modicum of wisdom. That is possible here.

If I have the courage to finish this small volume, it will not alone be the recording of my story, but the hope of telling some truths and denying some falsehoods in the arts I love so well, which will spur me on.

INTRODUCTION

While the chapters will not be designed to proceed on a logically ageing basis, it will be found that prior place is given to narratives and personalities with some irregularity, but always with the view to their fitting more agreeably into the general composition. In the closing chapter I shall feel able to speak with more candour than I have been able to use when speaking as P.R.A. and I shall not hesitate to criticise certain aspects of 'contemporary' art, nor to express disfavour of some tendencies of present day art-dealing, because I am certain that at their door lies a parcel of blame for a condition of sickness which time will show to characterise the painting and sculpture of our time.

CHAPTER ONE

BEGINNINGS

MY PARENTS, who were patterns of veracity, so I have no reason to doubt their word, told me that I was born at Codsall in Staffordshire on a morning in the middle of March eight years before the tragic twentieth century saw the lurid light. I came just before the Ides of March and it was an unwelcoming day, cold they said, with snow lying deep upon the ground. The church tower could be seen from the bedroom window, below, the bucolic life of a tiny village took its leisurely way. I'd better confess, though I blush to do so, that a bronze tablet now marks the spot. When I was born, Codsall was a real village and one went there by train from the nearby town. There were no buses to take one there and cars were nearly as new to the world as I was. We stayed there for a few months only. Afterwards my birthplace became the village post office. We next went to live in Wolverhampton which is five miles away. Today the Wulfrunian boundaries embrace many of the rural acres and people live along the roads leading to them. (To concern itself with amenities a Codsall Civic Society has just been formed and I have become its president.)

Our new home was the one in which my first vague awareness of life penetrated oblivion. For it must have been there that the child looked up from his mother's lap into soft nut-brown eyes such as Rembrandt painted. The memory of this is, as far as I can recall, my initial visual experience and draws for me the first line upon the blank paper of nothingness making sense and form where before there had been none. As far as I am concerned here my entity began.

Dark hair as well as dark eyes my mother had at the time — so my recollection has it. She went white very early and I cannot again remember it except like tarnished silver. Associated with this indelible film is a recollection of utter benediction the like of which I have never since experienced. She was young and beautiful, about twenty-two I suppose.

I have no equivalent memory-picture of my father and my elder brother is the only other person of a vivid hue at the time, but there is a vague shape of a nursemaid which looms up sometimes. It is ample and benign. Brother 'Jacky' in our nursery is clear-defined. Of the nursery itself I remember little. I know it stabled a large rocking-horse and the next clearest object is a tin vessel with a long spout used, I think, to cure a bronchial disposition in Jack. I think it emitted fumes from a nozzle when something was burnt in it. Do my nostrils recollect a stink of tar? A very definite image remains of Jacky helping me to climb through a ground floor window and then there is a blank.

The second home was replaced by a third when I was not yet four. I remember collecting acorns from a tree in the small garden to give to my elder brother on his fifth birthday. That was as rare a present as any I have given since, so it seems. Scents are powerful reminders. Nostalgically comes still the smell of the damp autumn oak leaves I trod underfoot when only three years old. But no more of these fragrant adumbrations, but to the clear task I have rather foolishly undertaken.

Jeremiah Crowther was, like Juliet's nurse's husband, 'a merry man' — 'God rest his soul'. He had an endless fund of stories with which he would delight us children. His figure was stocky, his voice deep and sonorous. His glass eye — consequent upon an accident — fascinated us. The optician, he told us, offered him a more expensive one, but, he had protested, he could see just as well with the cheaper aid. The seeing eye scanned us appraisingly, we thought, while the other seemed to possess a twinkling personality of its own and the two dwelt together harmoniously in his kindly face. 'Comfort', by name and nature, was his wife. (I've not come across that name since.) When she was born names were habitually taken from the Bible or from the Kings and Queens of England. When I remember her she was shrunken and shrewd, but just and upright as any Christian. In the house she usually wore a bonnet and woollen shawl as was the custom of elderly people in the Victorian age. While she maintained a gentle but firm discipline in her domestic realm Jeremiah was the undoubted lord and master. She 'knew' that when she died she would instantly meet her maker face to face. She had no doubt of it, for I once heard her declare that in preference to living she would choose 'to die tonight and meet my glorious Lord in the morning'.

These were my maternal grandparents. They were of the artisan class and he rose from the workshop floor to be works manager. They had ten children, the third of whom, Annie Florence, became my mother for it was she whom my father married when she was only 17, being 12 years younger than he. The Wheeler family thought she was a little below his station. But it was, on the whole, a happy marriage in spite of the snobbery of his mamma and sisters which my mother's disarming sweetness eventually overcame. It amused rather than troubled her.

My father's father I never knew for he died young of a chill contracted from sitting out late upon the lawn. He was a free-lance journalist and founded the firm my father carried on when he died. I was named 'Charles' after him and now have his heavy gold pocket watch engraved with seemly sentiment: 'A token of love to a precious father from his children, Wolverhampton 1881.' Many a flourish adds to its period charm. He must have been 'successful' because my father would proudly tell us children that his income once touched a thousand pounds. This in the nineteenth century was a notable sum. But that would be the peak of the family fortune and my father's income was small. The rise of Press Associations and Agencies cut the ground from beneath the feet of the free-lancers. Two of my father's employees I remember for different reasons. One named Burridge was a hero to us children for he was a soldier in the Boer War and when he came home on leave his scarlet uniform and his accoutrements made us boys goggle-eyed. The other, named Pendrel-Brodhurst, later became a London editor and leader writer. He was the last of his line to enjoy a government pension awarded to an ancestor who had sheltered King Charles in the Boscobel Oak.

Because my father had little money we had to take great care of our clothes and we lived frugally but adequately. We were not sent to Public School and only my younger brother attended Grammar School. The house we lived in was simple and comfortable enough for the family of five boys and a girl. Our childhood was disciplined and happy. I have always been glad of this for throughout my life I have learned that without discipline there is little happiness *and no great art.*

While my mother was an angel of goodness my father was intelligent and loved beautiful things. He made a small collection of Chinese porcelain. She tried to teach us to be good, he tried to teach us to be clever. If they did not succeed it was not because they were not commendable examples themselves. She was beautiful when young and lovely till she died of cancer before she was 60. As a child I thought it was worth being poorly to be nursed by her. It was with an unforgettable sense of security that I was wrapped up in a warm brightly coloured rug and tucked up on the sofa when sickly. Father was handsome, inclined to be sandy and superlatively cadaverous. He was something of a local character so unconventional in his manners and habits as to cause us children embarrassment. Children like conformity. Sam Phipps (my father, of course) was sometimes harsh but never, I think, intentionally unkind, though he revelled in scoring a point. Of the two she was the stronger character and ruled, as her mother did, supreme over all household affairs. He was a member of the Nonconformist Church, knew his Bible and could contend on Doctrine and Theology. She was the essence of goodness, lived up to the Sermon on the Mount and on the whole seemed content with that. We all

1. Prince Birabongse of Siam and the author with a bust of Prince Chula.

2. The author in working clothes being painted by his wife.

3. A light-hearted moment at Burlington House with Mr Zimenko, the Russian art historian.

4. The author with Sir Winston Churchill when the latter attended his last Academy banquet. On the same evening he announced his retirement from politics.

5. The P.R.A. discussing Academy matters over lunch with the Secretary, Mr Humphrey Brooke.

6. The author greeting the Queen and Prince Philip at Burlington House.

7. *Surrey Downs:* landscape

8. *Mother and Child:* chalk
drawing.

attended Lea Road Chapel on Sundays and I became an ardent Sunday School teacher there. I think it was a prevailing smugness among members of the chapel which eventually damped my enthusiasm for church-going.

My sister Evelyn, whom we named 'Little Mother', was spoilt and spoiling. She managed her five brothers exceedingly well and took the rough treatment she received, when we were very young, all in good part. She was sent to the best seminary for young ladies in the town and studied the piano, becoming later a distinguished teacher of music. She was the third child, I the second. My eldest brother Jack was 18 months older than me and not so many months separated the coming of each child till Stanley, the youngest, who was five years younger than Victor, the fifth. Frankland, who followed Evelyn, went to Canada in his teens to farm but became a Congregational minister; and Victor, following him to America, decided to stay and become an American national which he now is, living in Nebraska. All my brothers served in the first World War. A heart condition following rheumatic fever kept me out of hostilities.

Few families grow up more happily than we did and there can be few who have had less discord than we have had. The house which was our home for the best part of our growing-up was in Goldthorn Terrace — a well built, simply designed row of about a dozen, brick-constructed, mid-Victorian dwellings. (Not having a bathroom, we were tubbed in a tin bath before the kitchen fire of a Saturday night. That was a splendid way to bathe. As I write I can almost feel the ruddy glow of firelight on my limbs and the warmed towel placed round my body as I was dried before the fire.)

The house stood well back from the road with a field between. Elevated on high ground, it was approached by a long gravel walk lined on the one side with Lombardy poplars and being open to the field on the other. A flight of stone steps led to the terrace. I developed a great affection for these tall trees, the waving of their tops against the sky always gave me peculiar pleasure and many a time did I draw and paint them. Behind the terrace was a drive exactly 100 yards long down which we boys would sprint striving always to shorten the seconds. The drive and field in front together made our playground. I suppose the field was about three acres in extent and undulating. It had romantic hollows and mounds. In wet weather a pool developed in the lower contours and on this we made slides in the winter when it froze. I knew every inch, every little up and down, where all the tallest grasses grew, which part to avoid at nettle time and from where to gather the dock leaf to ease the sting when it came. I can recall the exact point on the terrace where the smallest jump would make the easiest approach and at what part it was too high to attempt the jump even for lusty and reckless boys who had all they wanted and found life full and exciting.

We faced westwards across the Penn Road about one mile south of the centre of the town — Wolverhampton. That we looked to this point of the compass is important because from the vantage place of our dining room window we could see right in front of us the Wellington Wrekin, that solitary mountain in Shropshire standing on the horizon twenty miles away. Its smooth curved symmetrical silhouette showed like a segment of a great bun with a small bite taken out at the top. Over the fields the housetops in the middle distance, the lines of trees behind, and rolling country beyond, the Wrekin stood majestically. By observing its tone and colour we could foretell the next day's weather with as much certainty as now we do by listening to broadcast forecasts. But most of all it had a place in our affections because of the superb sunsets which so often threw it into dramatic relief.

We all loved the skies. Both our parents loved them and taught us from our earliest years to marvel at the ever changing pictures of sky and cloud painted by the angels daily and hourly as on a canvas before our eyes as we looked through that memorable window pane — a large piece of glass taking the whole of the lower sash without glazing bars. Any one of us would call to the others 'Come and see this sky'. The setting sun was a common wonder, and a constant delight.

Before and below the backcloth of sky and distance, never forgetting the Wrekin, the panorama of daily life passed upon the 100 yard long stage of the Penn Road. At the wings stood on the left side the Royal Orphanage (now the Wolverhampton School), and on the right side the tall poplar trees. One of the principal actors was the family doctor — with the six of us his appearances were frequent. He would make his entrance from the right, get down from the trap he had been driving and handing the reins to his coachman would receive in exchange the little black bag with a rounded top, the indispensable prop of his profession. Doctor Hamp was a benign Victorian medico, the family G.P., and more beloved than 'Doctor Fell'.

Then of a summer's morning would at last appear before waiting juvenile eyes, from the poplar wing, the four-wheeler or 'growler' cab which had come to take us to the railway station. This was exciting indeed for it meant the beginning of holidays for us at Rhyl; but not before it was piled high with Saratoga trunk, boxes and portmanteaus and packed tightly inside with small children with knobbly knees and a couple of adults voluminously skirted. Broughams, tradesman's carts, and bicycles (before the free wheel) joined in the passing show. Sometimes a man with a dancing bear (I can still hear the clanking chains) and sometimes an organ-grinder with his scruffy monkey (I can still see him scratching the flea-bites) appeared on the bill. Characters such as tiny Mrs Pardoe, the nice housekeeper from next door, with her string bag of groceries and numberless other parcels would walk on, meeting in the middle the nurseryman Tom B. Dobbs who wore a scarlet waistcoat into the armpits of which he would thrust his thumbs and waggle his fingers (this was his gimmick) while he conversed with Mrs P. He ran a nursery behind the Terrace in which we were free to walk and where he kept a chained fox. Mr Bigwood's great Newfoundland dog was among the many actors who strutted their little hour upon the stage. And I must not forget Councillor Fred Evans who wore a cloth cap and had a blatant voice with which he would loudly declare: 'Best potatoes, cabbages, bananas, pears, apples — oranges likewise.' One of us once asked him what 'likewise' was. Evans was a greengrocer whose weekly appearance with his colourful pony cart was a major item on the programme. He later became Mayor of the Borough which in later years conferred its Freedom on me, who was one of his greatest admirers and most modest of customers.

Then there was the open-topped, horse bus which several times a day passed from left to right and right to left; and whose oil lamps flickered at night as we peeped through the curtains and out of our bedroom window, on hearing the horses' hooves, to see it pass. I recollect the driver with his long whip ever at the ready and his faded black bowler hat made greenish by age and weather, pulled tightly down over his ears. A heavy brown rug used to be wrapped closely around his ample frame, high up above his waist, almost to his armpits and at the other end over his boots. He was girded against all weathers. We boys were thrilled if we were allowed to be on the top front seat, lean over the iron rail and have him speak to us.

The actors came and went ceaselessly, though upon a road which carried a mere fraction of the traffic which now rushes across its macadam surface. Clouds of dust tailed behind the horses and carts, the broughams, traps and cabs which were the general means of transport. Their pace was quite enough. It was leisurely as became the era when Queen Victoria sat serenely upon the throne of an 'Empire on which the sun never sets'. And we were young, scarcely knowing what fear was, nor apprehension nor care.

One never-to-be-forgotten day — I must have been four years old — we were sitting in our stalls looking out on to the stage when a monster appeared. Excitement was intense as it entered from the orphanage wings and with fumes issuing from its nostrils groaned its hesitant passage from left to right to disappear behind the poplar trees. It was preceded by a character carrying a red flag (it was an ensign without political significance in those days), a thing we had only seen before when a steam roller came into view. My father told us the dragon was called a 'horseless carriage' and when we had recovered our senses we laughed loudly at so absurd a thing. Just a joke we thought. Of course we could not have guessed how mighty this apparition would become in the twinkling of an historic eye and who could have prophesied what a juggernaut. At that time it is doubtful whether Mrs Bridget Driscoll, supposedly the first victim of the motor car in England, had yet been killed. Now it claims 20 dead bodies every day upon our island's roads. Very occasionally we were horrified to hear someone had been trampled to death on the roads by a horse who had bolted. I remember seeing one such charge across our stage, with reins dangling wildly, dragging behind him an empty rattling cart. While the owner was shopping, the horse, left standing, had been frightened by a motor car. This was before the doomed cart horse had become accustomed to the look and sound of his iron rival and eventual exterminator.

Changes during my lifetime are certainly legion. My father once tried to explain to us the meaning of 'an atom'. We were sitting at dinner and, taking a crumb of bread lying on the table, he cut it in half. Then he halved the half and explained that if this process were to be continued to the limit of practicability the resultant speck would be an atom — i.e. an indivisible unit. Little did I imagine then that, later in my life, the splitting of the atom was to come about and that this new discovery makes possible the dissolution of the great globe itself, 'yea', and all that it inhabit'. Little did I imagine when as a boy I heard that the Wright brothers had actually left the ground in a heavier-than-air machine, that aeroplanes would compete with trains and ships and might even supersede them altogether. Little did I imagine when as a boy I read H. G. Wells *First Man in the Moon* that so fantastic a story would ever come true and yet before I die I may talk to a man who has been to the lunar satellite and returned unscathed to earth. And there is also the then unthought of television and music all

day long at the turning of a knob. All we had of tinned entertain-
ment was the magic lantern and the phonograph—the instrument
with a long trumpet like the one the fox terrier sits by in the
well-known advertisement. On the machine we placed cylinders,
not discs, which commenced with a very nasal voice: 'This is an
Edison Bell record.' We were happy without the wireless and
content without the 'telly'; and sometimes I echo John Skeaping's
words when we were buying lovely Provençal pottery near St
Remy and his eyes caught sight of some plastic 'replicas' — 'I hate
progress, Charles, don't you?' Progress has meant the canning of
other things besides music. When as a boy I used to go to the
grocers with my mother treacle came from a tapped barrel and
was poured into a 2 lb jam jar taken for the purpose; and sugar
was scooped into a blue paper bag deftly made by the grocer into
a cone-shaped receptacle while he was busy gossiping.

My mother had a soft contralto voice and would sing hymns
and popular drawing room songs to us accompanying herself on
the piano. It made her happy if we, with our little squeaky voices,
would join in. We all had lessons in piano playing and teachers
came to the house to give us dancing lessons. We would much
rather have played marbles than learn the steps of the polka. My
father was not musical as I remember him although he would sing
hymns vociferously because — they were hymns.

He preferred to read to us. His bookshelves were open for any
of us to take down the volume we fancied and it made him happy
to see us reading. He would reach for a book and read aloud in a
clear, incisive voice pausing from time to time to comment or
explain. He chose for us classics like Dickens, Carlyle, Samuel
Johnson, Milton and of course Shakespeare. My interest in
literature commenced with these readings as did my reverence for
great men and I recall the sensuous feeling of handling one of his
large leather-bound volumes of Shakespeare. It was from reading
its large type that I got my first inkling of the marvel and magic
of words, their music and their power. I began to realise that they
could paint pictures, record important happenings and stimulate

thoughts. And even then they often seemed to me to be very beautiful. Incipient awareness all this, in truth, but a deep impression was made then on a small teenager. Many other things I found on my father's shelves, dictionaries, Latin primers, atlases, sermons of Scottish divines, poems of Burns and Thomas Hood. These shelves were in the dining room which had the window of which I've been speaking.

The room contained other memorable things two of which, together with an object in my father's bedroom, I must mention because they fed my growing appetite for drawing and modelling. First there was a pair of anonymous landscapes in oil. Not great paintings, but done with a skill which fascinated me. I never tired of examining them. Secondly I was intrigued by an embossed panel in the Renaissance style on the brass coal skuttle and this I drew very often. And the object from the bedroom was a pottery bust of a Nonconformist preacher of the nineteenth century whose name I've forgotten, but I think it was Henry Ward Beecher. I tried to copy it in clay. This was the first experiment I undertook in sculpture.

My schooling was meagre in the extreme though I loved it all and would run to school in my eagerness. I remember some of my masters affectionately — the headmaster of St Luke's Elementary School to which I first went was benevolence itself. He wore a top hat, as also the doctor did. We did not fear, but respected him. Then there was 'Papa' Sheldon who taught us English at the Higher Grade School. He did not wear a top hat, not being 'grand'. He was shy and nervous and was mercilessly teased by his pupils. I will tell here of other cruelties pupils at the school would sometimes inflict on each other. I suffered agonies when I was put 'on the rack' just for fun it would seem. The procedure involved the seizure of a victim by three boys who would drag him to a buttress of the surrounding wall of the school playground. Number one and two would each take hold of an arm while number three heavily pressed the sufferer against the 'rack'. Then one and two would raise one foot against the return face of the buttress, to get leverage and placing the other firmly on the ground would pull the arms of the tortured wretch with all their might until he would yell for release.

As was to be expected my father raised many objections when I told him that I wanted to leave school before I was 16 to go to Art School. He, of course, saw the foolishness of this. I, of course, did not. But, as I have already said, he was unconventional and liberal minded. I was stubborn. A tussle ensued, but with my mother's aid I won the day. Mother did not realise the value of education as father did and she usually gave way to me in the end if I became heated over any matter. She feared agitation was harmful for my heart.

She was over-concerned about my health because of a serious illness I had when about 11 years old. I then became so ill following rheumatic fever that I was 'given up' by the doctors. 'If the doctors have given him up', she said, 'I will take on responsibility from now on.' She urgently sent to Flemings, the chemist in Queen Square, for leeches which sucked the poison from round the heart (their bite marks remained on my chest to this day to testify to their Aesculapian skill). To the amazement of everyone I began to get better. At my lowest ebb — the story goes — I protested that 'I don't want any more of those little fishes on me'. This remark appealed to her simple sense of fun and she would repeat it in the family, but never did I hear her boast that she had succeeded where the medical profession had failed.

My natural tenacity, my mother's fear of my being disturbed because of the condition of my heart, and my father's liberalism all contributed to the ending of my schooldays and the beginning of my long studentship in Art. At this point I am glad and thankful to be able to say that I received only encouragement from my parents, for this is by no means the common experience of those who take up this hazardous profession. And I have been conscious of another piece of good fortune for, in spite of my dangerous illness and its implication that I should suffer from a weak heart, I have had very good health ever since. It is true that I had to exercise some caution till I was twenty, but, when at that age I came to London, signs of a rheumatic condition which would sometimes stiffen my shoulder or leg began to disappear and since the ending of my studentship I have had no return of such a tendency. Being made a little nervous about my heart by an anxious mother I took precautions against physical strain, but as I used heavier and heavier carving hammers and chiselled more and more marble and stone, less and less did I need have cause for caution because this heavy work seemed to suit me; during my long career I have carved, I suppose, a hundred or more blocks of stone. By the mere raising of a 3-lb hammer during the course of a normal eight hours work I calculated once to have lifted 30 tons during the day and this took no account of the energy required to bring down the hammer on to the head of the chisel with sufficient force to overcome the resistence of solid rock.

But I go too fast. I had left school too soon but how transported was I when I became a real art student and how the smell of the studios blest my nostrils. I could not get to the Art School early enough each day nor stay too long at night. We began our studies at 10 a.m. and with breaks for mid-day dinner and tea (both being big meals) continued till 9 p.m. Unwillingly I had to leave ten minutes earlier in order to catch the horse bus about which I have written already, in Skinner Street. It is with nostalgia I think of these first days of my studentship. The intense whiteness of the great arc lamps — brighter than any artificial light I have worked by since — with their white-washed eight foot diameter shades in the antique room which illumined every detail of the plaster figures of Venus de Milo, the Discobolus, the Dancing Faun, Germanicus and so on, was replaced at nine o'clock by flickering yellow shafts thrown on to my fellow passengers in the Penn bus; cold classicism giving way to warm humanity with faces lit by small oil lamps — the blaze of illumination changed to Rembrantesque chiaroscuro.

Sometimes on wet nights I would wrap up on the open top, pull the tarpaulin sheet over me while the bus jogged along over

the cobbled Worcester Street and Penn Road passing the gaslit
street lamps, their flickering lights glinting in the gutter puddles
till we reached the Orphanage and I descended to be greeted at
home with a dish of boiled onions which my mother invariably
had waiting for my supper because they were 'good for you' and
which I devoured — they were delicious — by the light of another
oil lamp: we had no gas or electric light in our house at that time.
It was a handsome table lamp set atop a Corinthian column of gilt
metal and with a large engraved glass globe round a clear glass
'chimney' which shielded the flame from draughts.

I could sometimes persuade Thomas Eutychus Whittle, the
friendly caretaker, to let me in at the back door of the School on
Saturdays or holidays so that I could continue with my beloved
drawing and modelling. I remember well one Bank Holiday
when, working in the basement studio, I noticed a boy's head
thrust through a stone balustrade to peer down into the modelling
studio. Then I heard yells as he tried unsuccessfully to extricate his
tousled head, but not before a policeman had found a mason to
cut away the bulge on the baluster did the moaning cease.

Thomas Eutychus — it was only after many enquiries that we
found his original namesake had fallen out of a window while
listening to St Paul preach, was killed and was restored by the kiss
of life — was a colourful character. He had a large hooked nose
and birdlike eyes and was never seen inside or out without an old
cloth cap pulled well down over ears which stood out almost at
right-angles to his cheeks. He did anything and everything in the
school with good humour. Whether it were cleaning windows,
changing the carbon rods in the arc lamps, doing carpentry,
mounting drawings, casting in plaster, etcetera, etcetera, a rude
efficiency and willingness characterised it all. There was no
restrictive practice in Tom's tool bag and we were all fond of this
lovable little man with a Black Country accent you could 'cut
with a knife' as we used to say.

Most of my fellow students became art teachers, one going to
Roedean, one to Brighton, one to Sherborne and the cleverest of

them all to Epsom. This last — Percy Padden — had the appearance of a young Raphael and, so I thought, a like skill. Had he had greater tenacity and more luck he would have made for himself a considerable reputation. I remember clearly an exceptionally good watercolour he painted of a bath towel hung to dry on a clothes horse before the fire.

As for myself, after passing an absurdly large number of examinations from Historic Ornament to Modelling the figure from Life, and from Principles of Design to Perspective, I was lucky enough to gain one of the ten National Royal Exhibitions to the Royal College of Art. This was before local government authorities gave numerous and ample grants. My name was first on the list and for the next three years — it turned out in the event to be five — I received the finest instruction possible and £50 a year on which I thought I was 'passing rich'. My father said the world was at my feet, my headmaster, J. J. Brownsword, said 'Remember you don't know everything' and so I left home and art school on my way to London following the path well worn by the sandals of a multitude of pilgrims to the metropolis who have aspired to fame. I arrived, not without pale trepidation, but with a lively and confident hope.

CHAPTER TWO

CHELSEA

IT WAS EARLY in October, 1912, then that yet another 'young hopeful' came to London to seek his fortune. I had started on a great adventure with a mixture of apprehension and elation. At the Royal College of Art I joined up with another freshman, one Albert Wallace Peters, a brilliant student of painting from West Bromwich. He went to the war, was wounded, came back and died in the 'Spanish 'flu' epidemic of 1918. Had he lived he would have accomplished great things. He and I shared 'digs' together within a short distance from the College and were comfortably accommodated — bed and board for fifteen shillings a week — and as our scholarships provided us with a pound a week, five shillings remained with which to buy our lunch and working materials. All this was practicable 55 years ago.

It is not possible for those who had not the good fortune to live before the Great War to appreciate the atmosphere of well being and security which then prevailed. By following a planned course one felt sure of arriving at a certain goal. There were fewer snares and pitfalls then than now. I have lived in two worlds — before 1914 and after, and the first was nearer to heaven than the second. But maybe I am mistaken. Is there here a distortion of distance which causes the good things to be remembered and the bad ones forgotten? I really do not know.

Among the many new friends we made in the Common Room one stands out from the rest — Fred Richards — 'Dickey' as we called him. He was a Welshman up from Newport, Monmouthshire. He was older than the average newcomer because he had been a teacher in a boy's school there and had given up that career to become an artist. Dickey was a Celtic romantic oozing charm, and kindly with a smiling face and curly dark head of hair, thinning a little. He was careful and clean in dress, not eminently an art student characteristic then and far less so now. He specialised in etching and lettering, was a pupil and friend of Sir Frank Short and was active in all College social affairs.

To our great surprise some time in the 1920s he gave up art, became a representative of a British business house in Persia, selling motor cars I believe, but wrote and illustrated a book on the country while living there. One foggy Sunday night in November in the early 1930s while carving in my studio, I heard a rattling of my gate and peering through the gloom found a policeman and Dickey whom I had not seen for ten years. He gasped: 'I'm back in London, didn't know where you were, but with the help of this officer, have at last found you out — I was determined to do it.' We spent a memorable evening together. Very shortly after that he died.

Through his avuncular interest in Peters and me, we were persuaded to leave our digs and take a tiny unfurnished flat in Hereford Buildings. The rent was 5s. per week and for this we had a self-contained sitting room and bedroom with balcony front and back and rooftop with growing plants. Mrs Binder did for us for 2s. 6d. a week, washing and mending a few pence extra.

One approached the flat — it is still there opposite the Rectory gardens — through a pointed brick archway from Old Church Street, Chelsea, turned right up two flights of stone steps then out onto a long balcony from which one gained access to three or four separate dwellings. Ours was the last but one and entered by lifting up a latch and stepping into the living room. This faced to the balcony and was small, light and comfortable, warmed in winter by a gas fire and accommodated with fitted-in cupboards which were our 'larder' and 'pantry'. The lifting of another latch and the bedroom appeared, then in its turn, a latched door led to a tiny balcony on which our privy was located (we had a wash-hand stand made from two orange boxes prettily draped in willow-pattern chintz which my mother made). A few yards from the bedroom window were stables where dray horses by means of a long ramp were brought to their quarters immediately opposite so that our sleep was frequently disturbed by the restless hooves of horses kicking in their stalls. Dray-horses were still drawing wagons in London streets then, before the motor lorry dominated the road. My early blocks of stone came to Chelsea from Battersea by means of 'Artiss Pony' so said the delivery note.

These artisan dwellings were an experiment in nineteenth-century social welfare. As small flats they were designed extremely well for light, air and privacy. Of the many flats I have since visited built with like intention there is none which to my mind is more excellent even though advanced in modern equipment. Bathrooms were not thought to be essential then as now. But I think we kept ourselves clean. With the daily aid of a sponge and a weekly visit to the Chelsea Baths.

Fred Richards already tenanted one of the flats. Pieces of furniture began to arrive from our parents and we bought a few antiques at very low prices from Mr Grimsdall's shop situated on the ground floor of Hereford Buildings and facing Church Street — Grimsdall was a truculent little cockney antique dealer. There were few of them in Chelsea when I first lived in it. King's Road and Fulham Road are now thick with them. Grimsdall was an honest trader, content with a very modest living and standing no nonsense. An American customer on one occasion so offended him by arguing about price that he put a notice in his window reading: 'Americans need not apply.' When I asked if £1 was not too much for a Chinese dish I wanted he replied: 'Why — there are 15s. worth of rivets in it.' Richards, Peters and I would often edge into his shop loaded with stock and spend hours 'philosophising', listening to gossip and Grimsdall's catalogue of reminiscences. He had been a prizefighter in his youth and, thinking that as artists we would appreciate it, he would often punctuate his conversation with 'I strip well you know', and had to be discouraged from so doing behind an antique dresser.

Very soon we were established in sufficient comfort surrounded by our own possessions and experiencing a new freedom.

Within a stone's throw lived numerous artists who had 'arrived'. This was stimulating to us who thought we were 'on our way'. Charles Shannon and Ricketts had their studios in The Vale and so did Tonks. Wilson Steer, John Tweed, Walter Russell and Ethel Walker lived in Cheyne Walk, Henri Gaudier-Brzeska, Kathleen Scott and R. O. Dunlop at the 'Sign of The Hurricane Lamp' were near neighbours. Peter Scott was a boy of five. He would ride his tricycle up and down Church Street and below our windows, always scantily clad but a picture of vigorous health. I did not know his mother then, but later we became great friends both professionally and socially. During the second World War we often had musical evenings at Leinster Corner, the house where James Barrie once lived. Then, of course, there was Augustus John. I can see him now walking with a not unbecoming hauteur beneath the plane trees — still there — near the workhouse — no longer so called, and opposite the Town Hall. He is tall, erect and broad-shouldered, wearing a loose tweed suit with a brightly coloured bandana round a neck which holds erect, compelling features — not unlike, indeed very like, the traditional countenance of Jesus Christ. His etchings of himself when young show this. He is red-bearded and has eyes like those of a bull, doubtless is conscious of being the cynosure of the gaze of all Chelsea and looking neither to the left nor the right strides on with big steps and at a great pace towards Sloane Square, focussing on the distance and following, one imagines, some beautiful creature he is intent on catching up with. After opening a small exhibition of John's at the Upper Grosvenor Gallery last year (I am writing this in 1966), Mrs John wrote me the following letter which suggests that I remember him correctly:

My dear Charles, I must thank you for your splendid opening speech. It was very touching too, and brought back the early days when he was a dashing arrogant figure. It was nice to see your wife again. Will you give her my regards.

Very gratefully yours,
Dorelia.

Another picturesque figure in Chelsea in those days was Ellen Terry. I saw her only once but was struck by the gaiety, grace and charm of this ageing, but still lovely, actress as she left her house in the King's Road near Glebe Place and got into an open motor car. She wore a large hat with a veil placed over it pulling down the brim, and tied beneath the chin. As a harmony in grey she might have been painted on canvas by Whistler. But she was real enough and, equipped against dust and wind, drove off merrily, as I remember, that late afternoon westwards along the King's Road into the golden glow of the setting sun. I did not see her in Chelsea again.

Speaking of Whistler turns the 'inward eye' on to the image of Walter Greaves. The story was that he had been the boatman who had rowed Whistler on the river from where he sketched, that later he became a studio stooge and then took to painting. He was one of the Chelsea characters and the butt of rude little boys. He wore a tall and battered silk hat with square-cut frock coat and concertina-ed, pin-striped trousers. His boots were always immaculately polished — turning up a little at the toe-cap — and his hair oily and ebony black hanging in serrated locks over his coat collar. Grimsdall used to say he did them both with the same brush and at the same time. However, he would buy his drawings. Greaves had a down-at-heels appearance as, detached and flat-footed, he plodded along Church Street, Cheyne Walk, Paulton's Square, Glebe Place, King's Road and all that part of Chelsea we considered to be the hub of our universe. His coat was greenish black, like the bowler hat of the Penn bus driver, and was surely made for someone else. The tattered portfolio he invariably

9. *Mother and Child:* Bas
Relief — Portland stone.
National Gallery,
Wellington, New Zealand.

10. *Wings:* oil-
painting exhibited
at the R.A. (1940).

11. Professor Edouard Lanteri.

12. *Madonna and Child:* at Winchester College War Memorial Cloister.

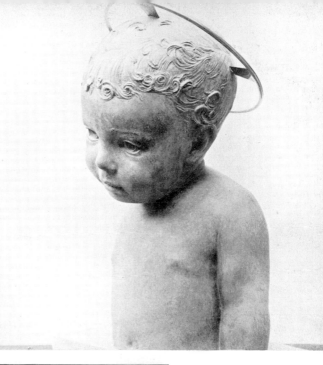

13. *Infant Christ:* at the Tate Gallery.

14. *Man and Woman:* Portland stone.

15. *The Family:* pinewood relief.

16. Design for the 'King's Medal' made for Prince Louis of Battenberg.

17. Angel, bronze detail: at the Bishop Jacob Memorial Church, Ilford.

carried also may have belonged to another artist, J. McNeill W. perhaps, but was always full of drawings of the riverside of earlier days; for when I remember him he was very old with a wizened face and thin, drooping moustache, like those of mandarins painted on Chinese vases. He would hawk around his sketches for a few shillings each. Only after his death were his pictures properly valued and I recall the shock and delight when first I saw his *Hammersmith Bridge* painted in his teens. None of us knew of his canvases and he was a figure of some amusement, but he kept 'the even tenor' of his way. We should have been incredulous if someone had ever said: 'There goes a considerable artist.' Yet so he was.

On Saturdays we etched at the College under Sir Frank Short, who like Lanteri was a craftsman *par excellence*, and Constance M. Pott, his assistant. Miss Pott, who lived to a great age, was indefatigable in her care for the students from the College who had gone to the war and she would spend all her evenings making up parcels of food and clothing comforts for the boys. Her particular prides were red flannel cummerbunds, which were referred to generally as 'dados round the dining room', and cod liver oil. While we were doing up parcels of a Saturday evening in her house in Brook Green, she would cook us a hot meal, but when we sat down to eat it she merely nibbled dry bread with perhaps a scraping of margarine. When she turned from talking of the boys and of etching she would discourse at length on how and why Bacon wrote Shakespeare! Apart from that she was sensible enough!

The Principal in these days was Augustus Spencer, a portly Yorkshire man with a deep gruff voice. He had a special gift for remembering names. After they had been in College for a week or so he knew the name of every freshman. This aptitude I should have found invaluable while I was P.R.A., but it has utterly escaped me. 'Gussy' was ponderous, uninspiring and uninspired. The Professors in the four Schools made up for this deficiency, however. Beresford Pite held the Chair of Architecture, Professor

W. R. Lethaby of Design, Gerald Moira of Painting and Edouard
Lanteri of Sculpture. They were all artists of great distinction. The
first three fascinated us with their lectures and Lanteri with his
demonstrations. By modelling before us a portrait or figure from
life, or making anatomical diagrams, he effectively imparted
knowledge which his broken English could ill supply. I regret
that I did not keep a photographic record of these diagrams drawn
with dry clay on the oilcloth 'cages' used to cover up our clay
models to prevent them hardening. But I have not forgotten the
clarity with which they conveyed the structure of the human
frame.

Our daily routine was simple. Breakfasting together — Peters
and I and Dickey, in our flat or his, the walk to the College, a day
of exciting work in the studios and back each evening to make our
own supper and, after setting the world to rights by arguing, we
went to bed, satisfied that we had had a good day. This was the
general pattern. For breakfast we bought bacon (streaky) at
fourpence a pound, the rind from which together with a few
bones thrown in would make the stock into which we would put
pot herbs for our supper. 'Pot' herbs cost us one penny and
consisted of one potato, one parsnip, one onion and one carrot,
bought at the greengrocer's at the corner of Church Street and
Paulton's Square. When flush we would go to Plummers in Lower
Sloane Street where we could dine off three courses for one
shilling. A 'ladies portion' of meat would reduce the bill by
twopence. Of this Galahadian concession we sometimes took
frugal advantage. When *very* flush we would go to 'The Good
Intent', in those days situated under the tower of the old Church
in Lombard Terrace, a row of simple Georgian whitewashed
houses facing the river and knocked to smithereens by the same
bomb which utterly demolished More's church in the second
World War. At this retreat for the artists who had 'arrived', we
would see such as John or Hugh Lane — the latter hated spending
on food money he lavished on pictures. A three-course dinner
cost us one shilling and sixpence.

Dining within a stone's throw of Chelsea Old Church was wonderful and I shall never forget the sense of loss I suffered (which so many suffered) when I climbed over the heap of bricks the next morning after the bombing, a heap which had been, the day before, the pivot round which life had revolved for me so many years since I first arrived in Chelsea. That simple and noble brick tower at the bottle-necked end of Church Street seemed to stand at the heart of things and to have a special meaning for Chelsea — aesthetic, spiritual and sentimental — and I was glad when it was finally resolved to rebuild it as formerly. Now when I pass it I seldom recall that tragic night when it was struck down and turned to rubble, completely and utterly.

But I digress and must return to Hereford Buildings where coffee making after dinner was something of a ceremony. Friends came in to crowd our tiny sitting room and we sang and talked, putting, as I have said, all matters under the sun in their proper place and giving each their rightful value by the light of a smelly and smoky Roman lamp and the crude clarity of the unquestioning assurance of youth, until the small hand of the clock assumed the vertical and we bedded down, assuming the horizontal.

It was fortunate for me that having left the inspiring influence of Emerson of whom, more later, I should come to study under that great teacher Edouard Lanteri. He was brought to England from Paris by Legros and for about 40 years held the Chair of Sculpture at South Kensington. He was debonair, a pattern of courtesy and an undisputed master of his craft. If — after being under him for the usual Diploma Course of five years — one failed in the smallest detail of one's equipment as a sculptor then it was because one was stupid, or lazy, and if one failed in becoming an artist it was not his fault because the one can be taught, the other cannot. Prominent among his pupils when I joined his school were Charles Sargeant Jagger, who made the Artillery Memorial at Hyde Park Corner and the moving bronze soldier reading a letter from home which forms the Railways War Memorial on Paddington Station; Gilbert Ledward who sculpted the Guards Memorial on Horse Guards Parade and the fountain in Sloane Square; William McMillan who designed the Beatty Fountain in Trafalgar Square and the George VI statue in The Mall; Alfred Hardiman whose controversial equestrian statue of Haig stands in Whitehall and whose fine heraldic lions flank the entrance to the City Hall at Norwich, and James Woodford who sculpted the Queen's Beasts at Windsor.

As the war went on the Professor and I became great friends. I helped him teach in the studios and when his annual bout of bronchitis laid him low I was put in charge of the school. I also assisted him with his commissions in his private studio. He would habitually ask me to re-write his letters drafted in a delightful broken English. This I would do under protest because I was sure his correspondents would rather have had his charming version than mine, more 'correct' may be, but dull by comparison.

Although Lanteri had lived in England for so long, he could never master the language. I remember one delicious specimen. As he handed a pupil, for study, one of his personal plaster casts, he said: 'Der — and you will not break it if you can — won't you!' We all admired him and trusted absolutely in his guidance. When I was a student this pupil-master relationship was general. A half-century since has made a considerable difference. He was a venerable and undisputed master. He often used to say to me, 'Wheeler, none of us draw enough'. I believed him then, and now I know more surely how truly he spoke.

There was one occasion on which the pupil-master relationship almost broke down in my case. It was in 1914 when the great Ivan Mestrovic exhibition was held at the Victoria and Albert Museum. In one of his lectures to us, Professor Beresford Pite referred to the Serbian sculptor as 'genius in the gutter'. Since his many great sculptures in wood, bronze and marble had a profound impression on me I felt outraged at so defamatory a phrase. I half rose to my feet to protest, but not having sufficient courage, sat down again and so avoided being 'sent down'. Ever since I have blamed myself for Mestrovic is certainly one of the true geniuses of the twentieth century. The emotional peasant force of his work was too much for the polite society to which Pite was accustomed, but to me, and to some of my fellow students, it was a revelation of style, strength and profundity, new and exciting. I was very greatly affected.

I passed through the five year College Course in the normal way, gaining the Diploma in my third year. The war was ending and the Numismatic Society promoted a competition for medal designs, anticipating a post-war demand. I entered several models and was awarded prizes totalling £90. This was opportune coming at that difficult period when having completed training one stands on the uncertain threshold of a career. Lanteri called me to him and told me that with the money I had won I must get a studio and set up as a sculptor. His word being law I did as he directed and found my first studio just off Church Street in the shadow of Chelsea Old Church in Justice Walk. The Court Room and ancient lock-up were on the opposite side of the narrow passage. The famous Chelsea Pottery had stood upon the adjacent land. Another sculptor, one George Alexander, occupied the only other studio in the Walk. You will find both studios now turned into dwelling places as you will find many another studio in Chelsea converted to domestic use. Artists have been driven out by an affluent society moving westwards from Mayfair.

In the nearby Cheyne Row was a group of studios occupied by other young sculptors and together we formed a coterie with not dissimilar views and enthusiasms. There was William McMillan and Gilbert Ledward. Henry Parr and Charles Vyse were both making excellent pottery figurines. In Upper Cheyne Row A. G. Walker was sculpting the bronze statue of Florence Nightingale now on her pedestal suitably sited near the Crimean War memorial at the lower end of Regent Street. Leonard Merrifield was modelling the statue of Carson now in Belfast and Leonard Jennings sculpting horses there at the same time as Captain Adrian Jones was making, in Old Church Street, the huge models for the bronze Quadriga on the Wellington Arch. We all admired the seated bronze statue of Thomas Carlyle by Edgar Boehm on the embankment nearby and abstract sculpture had scarcely been thought of.

Here I was then, ten years after I had launched my vessel in Wolverhampton, with it riding hopefully on the high seas of Art in the heart of Chelsea. Forty pounds a year was the rent. But I had no commissions. I begged clay from the College; a banker or two I got for next to nothing. I had £50 to last me till something came along. This was in 1917. With the war coming to an end medal design was in the air. One day out of the blue I received a letter from Prince Louis of Battenburg asking if he could come to see me in my Hereford Buildings rooms. Whatever did this mean? I was on tenterhooks. When he came to my door he said: 'I'm an Admiral, you know, at present out of a job.'

Agitation by a prominent newspaper because of his country of birth, had forced his removal from Supreme Naval command, a post in which he was loved and respected by all ranks. If ever there was a white Englishman it was he. On our second meeting he told me he had changed his name to Mountbatten. The purpose of his visit was this. He had seen my medal designs in the competition when he had brought me the £90, liked them and wanted me to do designs for a Victory medal. He had been talking about me to the King who, realising how cumbersome would be the business at the end of the war of giving and receiving to and from each of the numerous Allies their respective war medals, as was traditional, had conceived the idea of having a general medal which should be common to all the countries in arms together and not require reciprocal exchange between them. He invited me to make the necessary designs for what he termed 'The King's medal'. For the obverse I designed a seated and winged figure of Peace above a crouching warrior, surrounded with the motto, *Reddita Pax Terris Debellatique Tyranni*. On the reverse was a circular chain with 12 links on each of which was the name of one of the Allied countries. This was based on a rough sketch by the Admiral. It was proposed to send photographs of the medal designs, when the King had approved them, to the Allied countries inviting them to accept the scheme. After many modifications my models were approved. In due course I sent the parcel of photographs to the Marquess of Milford Haven, as Prince Louis had then become, and received this brief acknowledgement on July 31st, 1917:

> Kent House,
> East Cowes,
> Isle of Wight.

Dear Mr Wheeler,
   Many thanks for the excellent photographs of your beautiful model. I wish us all success. Yours truly,
   Milford Haven.

They did not have the success he wished. All the Allies agreed save one — France — and so there the matter ended. It was subsequently agreed between the allied nations to adopt a general medal with a common subject for the reverse —'Victory'— and each country would produce its own designs and designers. William McMillan designed the British one.

Some little time after this abortive scheme a National competition was organised for designs for a plaque which it was proposed to give to the next-of-kin of soldiers who had been killed in the Great War. I entered several designs. Before the final result was announced it was widely rumoured that one of my models had been given first place. Now, thought I, I can end our long engagement. She had waited five years for me. Now was near, I believed, the consummation so devoutly wished for — because we should have enough money to marry on.

CHAPTER THREE

THE BRIDE AND
THE POET

WHEN THE RESULT was at last announced, however, Carter-Preston of Liverpool was placed first and I second. Instead of receiving a prize of £250 therefore I got only £100. This was a blow, because we had planned our marriage on the larger sum. Nevertheless, she agreed to marry me in spite of this.

I had met Muriel Bourne first when I was 16 and when we were art students together in Wolverhampton. She was very slender and straight like a young willow, had long dark hair hanging down the back to her waist and an ivory oval face with large eyes of the same colour as my mother's. When working in the studios she wore cotton print overalls which were always immaculately clean. She was light-hearted, had a merry laugh and was very gifted with her pencil and paint brush. She had artists as forbears, I had none that I knew of.

A great-uncle of hers was Herbert Bourne, the engraver, who engraved many plates of Gustav Doré's religious paintings and other plates for Queen Victoria. He lived to a great age. Longevity is in her family and when I first knew her she still had three nonagenarian grandparents living. Hugh Bourne, the founder of Primitive Methodism was an ancestor so that Nonconformity was always her family's religious practice.

Hugh was brought up as a Wesleyan, became a local preacher but was expelled from the denomination for his views. He had many followers, however, commonly called 'ranters' who, binding themselves together, adopted the title Primitive Methodist Connection. He was an indefatigable preacher and in the early nineteenth century made many preaching tours in Ireland and America with great success.

Muriel and I studied together in the Antique and Life rooms and in the same modelling studio, often working back to back. Sometimes we would collide in stepping back to look at our models.

This was the beginning of a life long devotion which has been undimmed and undivided from then till now.

I do not believe there is a kinder, sweeter, more unselfish creature in the whole of this sorry world, none more genuinely good. She has always been beautiful to me. My eyes have been ever delighted and my heart constantly gladdened because of her. This is not the stuff which makes love stories popular; they require to be more piquant. I have not been married more than once, nor had a series of amorous adventures. Our love life is a flower not grown in a hot house or flaunting itself in flower show tents. It is as a multitude of others are, not to be recorded in newspaper columns, but growing in green pastures, beside the still waters, not sensational but very lovely and smelling sweet. Our companionship has made life in its dark places more to be endured and in its light patches happier by far.

The £100 was about all I possessed and she married me on that in St Peter's Church, under the torture of whose practising bells we had sat many examinations together in the adjacent Wolverhampton Art School, and in whose lovely interior we had together made many drawings, labouring to improve our art. With what care and calculation we had to order our affairs few couples in these more affluent days can conceive. However, with pinching and her courage and care we got through some very lean times. We lived very simply and extremely happily, but I can remember one Sunday when we were invited to visit friends in the suburbs and we prayed for heavy rain so that we should have a valid excuse for not going. Between us we hadn't the pence for the bus fare. Fortunately it did rain. There was no sordidness in our lack, for we were young, fit and very much in love. We enjoyed a genteel poverty and envied nobody.

I was often tempted then to vacate my studio, save the rent and take a safe teaching job. I was well qualified for that, but when I spoke of it she would never listen. 'The last thing you do', she would say, 'is to give up your studio.' And so I held on till after about two years of Spartan living there was a knock one morning at the door of my Justice Walk studio. When I opened it, I saw a short man standing in morning dress and wearing a tall silk hat. My first thought was — here is someone selling encyclopaedias, and then he handed me his card. On looking I was so astounded that I handed it back to him. It read 'Rudyard Kipling'. I've ever since regretted my stupidity for his card would have been a thing to treasure as it brought relief, not before it was needed, and from that day to this I have never lacked commissions.

Kipling had been sent to me by Herbert, later Sir Herbert Baker. I had done a tiny thing for him on the torchiers of the Harrow School War Memorial. This had probably satisfied him and so he had suggested to the poet that I might make a bronze memorial plaque for his son John, killed in action at Loos at the age of 17. '*Qui ante diem periit*' as the inscription in bronze records. Rudyard and his wife 'Clemmie', as he called her, would come to see the model as it progressed. When any point of detail arose he always demurred to her opinion. The Kiplings were well pleased with the clay design. The only criticism was, I recall, his questioning a slackness in the ribbon binding the wreath of laurel. 'John would not have liked a loose strap,' he said; and so I tightened it.

The casting of this commissioned work brought me abruptly up against the difficulties a sculptor sometimes encounters in his dealings with his bronze founder, on whose faithful reproduction from the model he must depend. A very skilled, but in some ways not altogether reliable, founder (recommended by my professor) to whom I had entrusted the work, delayed and delayed until, the time being short, he was obliged to carry out hurriedly his contract to supply the bronze casting by the agreed date. The hurry was considerable and the casting consequently disastrous. Since I was committed to show the memorial tablet to my client, a large hole, which had appeared in the plaque, had to be patched, again hurriedly of course and again of course badly. Kipling spotted it at once, turned and enquired who was my bronze founder. 'An Italian named . . .', I replied. 'I don't know his lingo', Rudyard said, 'but tell him from me it's bloody'.

I undertook to have a new cast made, but I was angry that a founder should endanger my reputation even at the commencement of my career. Bronze-casting is an occupational hazard. It will be remembered that Benvenuto Cellini suffered agonies with the casting of his Perseus. When one is working to a deadline and a bronze turns out badly one is sometimes faced with the dilemma of whether to accept or reject the work. (This problem arose with two of the large groups I made for New Zealand. I solved it by having the bronze casts sent to my studio where by working myself with drills, hammer and chisel, files and abrasives for many weeks I restored them to the condition in which they should have left the foundry. The chasing of a good cast by the founder would have taken only a few days, but to make an entirely new cast would have taken many months. Disappointing as the bronzes were I derived great satisfaction from carving bronze, for it literally had to be carved in places, and in the re-patinating of the newly worked surfaces, as I also did from executing this complex commission in the three years agreed upon.)

The memorial tablet to John when finished was placed in Burwash Church. His parents then asked me to make, from photographs, a bust of the young lieutenant which they said they would inspect from time to time as I worked on it. In due course they were asked to come up from Batemans to see the portrait, but my letter received no answer, neither did a second sent some weeks later. In a third letter, guessing the reason, I suggested that perhaps they found it hard to face up to the sculptured image and if that were so I would destroy the work and call the whole thing off. This proved to be the case. Poor Kipling was utterly undone by his son's loss and never got over it.

I can recall many memorable things he said, but one I think I should record. He told me he had been consulted about the siting of the Cenotaph in Whitehall to which objections had been raised because of traffic considerations. He had come down heavily on the side of the Whitehallers because, he said, it would be right and proper that Prime Ministers on their way from Downing Street to the Palace of Westminster should be reminded, in passing, of their responsibility for the lives of the young men of the nation, which they held in their hands. When he came to see the tablet he would look at other work I was engaged upon. A portrait bust of my son, Robin, aged nine months, seemed to give him particular pleasure and he looked closely one day to see if I had put in the crease at the back of the neck which he said was such a lovely thing in a child's head. Years later he asked me: 'What are you going to make of that son of yours.' I replied: 'His mother and I don't mind much so long has he himself as a strong inclination for a particular career.' Kipling replied: 'Amen to that. Amen. So many people come to me and say "whatever shall I do with my boy?" '

I saw Kipling for the last time in France. We had been attending the unveiling by Generalissimo Foch of the Indian Memorial to the Missing at Neuve Chapelle, for which I had carved two tigers guarding the base of a tall column. After the ceremony a formal luncheon was given at Béthune. As we were gathering together many of our French hosts asked me to point out Kipling. They were not interested in Lord Birkenhead, the Secretary of State for India, nor in his speech, the most important of the occasion, but they *were* eager to see the poet and became entranced — we all did — by the words of Rudyard who, though not on the Speech List, was called to his feet and spoke without notes briefly and movingly about the bravery of Indian soldiers fighting on European soil. His earnest words silenced the restless feet and impatient murmurings so that you could hear the proverbial pin drop till he sat down to tumultuous applause.

The large Neuve Chapelle tigers were carved each out of a single block of Euville stone *in situ*. Euville is a free oolitic limestone good to cut especially in the 'green' state I received it. This of course applies to all freshly quarried stones, marbles and granites which on exposure to the air rapidly case-harden. Two assistants went over to France to rough-out the work and I arrived later to complete it. I was obliged to make frequent visits of inspection and on them to smuggle in from England a special brand of snuff without which, so he assured me, Johnson couldn't carve. Johnson, Wilkinson and I would stay at the local hostelry 'Auberge de la Bombe' where accommodation was rough and the food unmentionable. I shall never forget the *Potage d'Agriculture*! We often started work at 6 a.m. finishing at 6 or 7 p.m. These animals were the biggest sculptures I had undertaken up till then and I found tremendous exhilaration in chiselling those large forms, in a sympathetic material, well up in the clear and peaceful air. Sometimes I would eat my picnic lunch sitting in the corn fields while I listened to the whispering of the barley ears as they waved in the breeze over the land where earlier the Indian warriors, whose bloody sacrifice had caused the memorial to be erected, had fallen, and where later on I was to be lined up with others responsible for the making of the memorial, to be presented to Generalissimo Ferdinand Foch. He was remarkably small in stature as have been many famous soldiers.

The night before the ceremony I stayed at a hotel in Ypres where also were staying the members of the government, the War Graves Commission, the Indian and British Armies and so on. It was exciting to me to sit after dinner in the same lounge, though in a far-away corner, and gaze on these people of importance — getting V.I.P. treatment while I was tardily and seemingly grudgingly supplied with my coffee. I watched them from afar and saw them all go upstairs to make an early bed against the morrow's ceremonies. I remained only to see Lord Birkenhead come down again to return to his cups—alone. When I retired, the Secretary of State for India stayed where he was in solitary contemplation. His young daughter, Lady Pamela Smith, was making a name as a novelist then and the table plan at the Béthune luncheon next day placed me next to her. The Frenchmen at the table coming early altered the place names so that they could have the charming company of this talented lady while I was put far below the salt.

As I shall record in the course of my story, one of my earliest important commissions and the one which came between the John Kipling tablet and the tigers on the battlefield was to sculpt a Madonna and Child in the Winchester College War Memorial and overlooking the Meads. There was at Winchester at that time an art master, Richard Gleadowe by name. (He designed the Stalingrad Sword.) It was due to him that during the war, when he was advising the Admiralty about War Artists, I was commissioned to make busts of naval officers. He could draw exquisitely and was a friend we lost early in our married years for he died young, when he was well set and well equipped for a full life.

The Winchester Madonna had established for me a certain 'reputation' and my choice as the sculptor for the building of the Bank of England in Threadneedle Street was consequent upon my sculpture in the College meads. At the same time that I was executing the Bank commission I was also designing stone and bronze for India House and South Africa House, so that in addition to my Chelsea studio I was obliged to take another in Pembroke Walk in Kensington with Gilbert Ledward as a near neighbour and James Gunn next door. I am glad to remember how his charming Pauline, James and I used to gossip on our doorsteps when, after a day's work, we would go to the open door to see the sun going down of a summer's afternoon. From the day Kipling knocked at my first studio door till the bombs began to fall on London, i.e. for 20 years, I did not have an idle moment.

46

The last large job before the war was the Jellicoe Memorial Fountain in Trafalgar Square. William McMillan did the Beatty fountain there, both of us working sympathetically together with Edwin Lutyens as architect. Parliament commissioned us. The Commissioner of Works which dealt with such matters before the Ministry of Works was instituted, was presided over by Sir Philip Sassoon and he was a patron after my own heart, for he avoided bureaucracy as much as possible and made decisions whenever he could in the Medici manner of a benevolent dictator; and that works in matters of Art better than do democratic committees. He was obliged to show a model of the scheme in the tea room of the House of Commons, but, fearing delaying criticisms, he arranged for it to be placed there at 4 o'clock on the very day that the House rose for the summer recess and when Members were eager to get away. Having carried out at least the letter of the regulations and received no adverse opinion Sassoon told us to go ahead and by the time Parliament reassembled the matter was *un fait accompli.* This very handsome as well as wealthy official, so unofficious and disliking officialdom, was a live wire indeed and had a passion for fair and lavish things. He had a clear high-pitched voice but couldn't sound his r's. One day on coming in at the door of the studio and seeing Muriel at the other end, at the top of his voice he exclaimed: 'Oh Mrs Wheeler, what a pwetty fwock!'

In addition to a sympathetic Commissioner, McMillan and I were fortunate in having the whole-hearted backing of an enlightened Civil Servant in Sir Eric de Norman who pressed forward the commission and pushed difficulties on one side. Poor Sassoon died before the fountains were erected because, although it was planned to unveil them in 1939, the war came and the bronze groups were buried in the vaults of the British Museum for the duration.

When the war ended the sculptures were resurrected, placed in the already completed basins and a grand unveiling by the Duke of Gloucester was arranged. All the Services were represented with, naturally, Sea Captains predominating. McMillan and I had spent many hours experimenting with different nozzles in order to get the jets of water to our liking, but when the water was officially turned on there was consternation in the square. The reason for this was that Admirals, it would seem, do not like water and wildly stampeded when their best clothes were spattered with the sprays driven before a lively breeze into the posse of senior naval officers standing at the foot of Nelson's column. It may be that the water-engineer was a trifle too assiduous in the part he had to play in this tribute to the Royal Navy's heroes, but otherwise all went well.

This commission has given me a special interest in Trafalgar Square. When some few years later the proposal to erect in London a statue of Field Marshal Smuts was being discussed I wrote a letter to *The Times* suggesting it should be sited in the Square. I proposed that Chantrey's equestrian statue of George IV (the King without stirrups) could be moved from the eastern to the empty western pedestal leaving the one adjacent to South Africa House vacant. On this should be placed an equestrian statue of Smuts. This would have given London a chance for a last equestrian portrait and given symmetry to the north side of the Square. It is unlikely that soldiers will ride horses much longer and Smuts loved being on horseback.

On the day the letter appeared Jacob Epstein telephoned to say *he* had been asked to make the statue. I did not know this — it was not generally known — and after apologising I asked where his bronze was to be placed. He replied: 'In Parliament Square along with the other "stiffs".' I have wondered since if, wishing to avoid his statue entering the 'stiff' category, he did not deliberately give the figure that uncomfortable lean-forward which certainly marks it out from the rest of the great men whose company he has joined. However, the chance to give balance to Trafalgar Square's north facade has gone — perhaps for ever.

Though often requested to do so I have resolutely declined to take pupils, the real reason being that I have always been too

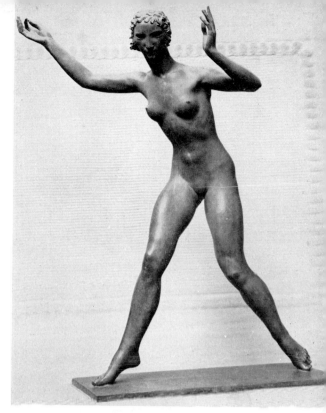

18. *Spring:* bronze statue at the Tate Gallery.

19. The Indian Memorial to the Missing, Neuve Chapelle.

20. Tiger in Euville
stone: detail of Plate 19.

21. *Art and Industry:*
group for the Franco-
British Exhibition in
Paris (1937).

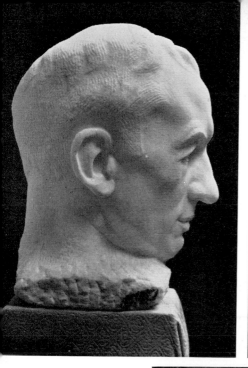

22. Sir Herbert Baker: marble bust in the Bank of England.

23. Portrait of the author by Muriel Wheeler F.R.B.S. Bust in lead.

24. The author and the Old Lady of Threadneedle Street.

25. Telamons carved *in situ* on the Bank of England (1930).

occupied with commissions. But there have been two exceptions. In my Justice Walk studio an American woman came to learn what I was able to teach her of sculpture. Her artistic accomplishments were rather slight, but her delightful personality attracted her to Muriel and me. She became a great friend and lived with us during the first years of the war. A lover of England she faced the bombs and refused to go to the States until, as she said, 'they send a warship for me'. They almost did, for she returned with English children sent to America for safety and escorted by ships of the United States Navy. As she lived in California we saw little of her since then, but corresponded regularly until she died not many months after Churchill, with whom she boasted equality of years. Elizabeth was a supreme optimist and as we sat under the stairs during raids and drank her own brewed 'American coffee' she would say, 'Aren't we having a good time', then CRASH, the bombs rained down.

She remained a spinster and her brother-in-law would say to her: 'A husband would be no end of a nuisance to you, Elizabeth.' He would like nevertheless to see the married Elizabeth with many children, for he declared she would have lined them up each morning and charged them to 'go away and be happy or I will beat you'.

The second 'exception' was Prince Birabongse of Thailand. His cousin, Prince Chula Chakrabongse, who was his guardian, told me that Bira wanted to learn sculpture. He was at Eton at the time, but had no inclination to proceed to the University. I agreed to take him as a pupil if he would undertake to work at least six hours a day for five days a week. The boy agreed to do this and kept his undertaking for three years, during which time he developed well. He worked hard and made some good busts and animal sculptures, one of which was bought by Gracie Fields for her garden in Hampstead. Another made a fountain in Bangkok. He was a curious mixture of the static and dynamic, the one fitting him for his studies, the other for his meteoric career as a racing driver under the name of Bira. This remarkable achieve-

D

49

ment on the racing track can be said to have begun in my studio and it came about in this way.

Prince Birabongse came of age while studying under me and Chula begged me to let him have his party in the studio — at some inconvenience, since it meant moving heavy stones and bronzes, converting the gallery into a musicians' platform, etc. There was the garden and the house, a warm summer's evening, Chinese lanterns, a fountain and flowers all making an ideal and unusual setting, with statues looking on. The high spot of the party was to be the arrival from Doncaster of a newly minted E.R.A. racing car brought to London by Raymond Mays. This was a present from Chula to Bira. The hour appointed was nine o'clock, but after much hectic telephoning, the machine came at last in the early hours of the morning and was run down a ramp into the courtyard. At that very moment all the lights went out, but my studio assistant, the resourceful Chadwick had prepared against this eventuality and dark consternation soon ended in applauded illumination.

All the guests were expected to christen the new thing by sitting in the driver's seat, in this case tailor-made to fit Bira. Some of us had dimensional difficulties, especially Mme Massine. (Massine with his Corps de Ballet were there.) Having squeezed in, the problem of getting her out was more difficult to solve. With the aid of gallants and much physical persuasion she was finally extricated, but not with her white satin dress remaining unimpaired. The anatomy of the young Siamese Prince and that of the maturing Russian ballerina were scarcely *en rapport*. When the festivities ended and as daylight came, the racing car was loaded on to a waiting lorry. Engineers travelled with it to Dover putting the finishing touches to the machine *en route*. It was shipped to France and Bira followed to win second place in his first big race at Dieppe. This was the initial step in a remarkable series of racing achievements. As these mounted, it was inevitable that his practice of sculpture should dwindle. I am given to understand that he now sculpts no more in Bangkok, but his interest in internal combustion engines remains.

The large contingent of the Russian ballet which came to Chelsea at midnight were in splendid form. They ate ravenously and gave an impromptu cabaret. Among the items Massine and Danilova danced to the Blue Danube waltz, Tamara Toumanova and Massine did a Spanish dance together with much verve and some little caution for the polished studio floor was more slippery than a stage.

King Prajadhipok, Bira's uncle, came one day to see his nephew's work and with him came the most beautiful woman I think I have ever seen, Queen Rambai.

The King asked me the usual question: 'What does a sculptor do if he knocks off a piece of stone he wants.' I gave the stock answer: 'He doesn't', to which he replied: 'We have a story of a man who took a log of a tree to make from it a canoe. He was a merry man who sang as he worked. He was not dispirited when one day he discovered he had cut away too much for a canoe. "Never mind", he said, "I'll make a paddle." When on another day he discovered the same mistake he was not abashed and chipped away — and, singing while he worked, made a wooden spoon.'

CHAPTER FOUR

HERBERT BAKER

OF HERBERT BAKER I hope this chapter will not unworthily tell of my admiration, affection and indebtedness. He was a proud 'Man of Kent', being one of a family of nine sons and two daughters and was born in the seventeenth-century house, Owletts at Cobham, in which, after more than eighty years of vigorous and creative life, he passed away.

His parents decided he should be an architect because 'he could draw' and he became a student in the Architecture School of the Royal Academy of which, of course, he later became a distinguished Academician. Failing to gain the Gold Medal and Travelling Scholarship, he found himself free, when the opportunity arose, to travel to South Africa and join his brother Lionel who had emigrated to fruit farm there. He took with him a dream — that he might become a successful architect in that 'land of promise' as he called it. He set sail in the first part of March, 1892 — maybe on the very day that I was born. If so, a day of great moment for us both. He amply realised his dream and I, a quarter of a century later, crossed his path. After that we walked many an exciting road together. One of the first was to Winchester where I was to carve a Madonna and Child.

This was the first time I climbed on to scaffolding and carved direct on a building. Since then I have laboured much, making architectural sculpture in blocks already built into the structure. This is the kind of work I have found to be most satisfying. The Winchester job was an exacting though a pleasant task. Muriel came down with Robin, my son, aged five and we lodged there for some weeks while the sculpture progressed.

This was during the headmastership of M. J. Rendall, that monumental teacher whose enthusiasm spurred us on and whose appreciation cheered and flattered us. The Cloisters scheme was the brainchild of both Baker and Rendall for they discussed together every detail of the design. They were men of the same years who, meeting first when they were over 56, seemed to enjoy a second boyhood together. One day when they were 80 I remember they linked arms and did a two-step on my studio floor while they chanted 'We are the octogints'. Rendall would come up almost daily on to the scaffolding on which I was carving. His large moustache, sparkling eyes and statuesque physique — I can see him now, and can hear his deep bass voice. He mounts the ladder, talks for ten minutes or so and descends, chuckling, to take his ample way across the soft, secure and immemorial lawns back past the Chapel to his house, leaving behind him a sense of well being and an it's-all-right-with-the-world flavour. Winchester College was 'Monty' in those days and 'Monty' was Winchester and both seemed as if they would remain as they were to the end of time. Rendall wrote this sonnet to Baker:

> *From Africa to England, where he wrought*
> *The great War-Cloister, with Imperial domes*
> *Telling of distant sea-enchanted homes,*
> *His crowning masterpiece of solemn thought.*
>
> *Boyhood was in his blood and here in truth*
> *He found his utmost theme, a host of names*
> *That burn to us who love them as bright flames,*
> *And stand apparelled in eternal youth.*
>
> *Yet learn the final secret of 'God's Acre'*
> *What time the sun harnessed his golden steeds,*
> *The Artist took fresh glory from our 'Meads',*
> *Chapels and Chantries: all adored their Maker.*

HIGH RELIEF

His past was not forgotten, but reborn,
When Wykeham met him on that summer morn.

When Monty retired he would visit me in my London studio. I was always fearful for his safety when he came to town. He seemed to have no idea of geography and would arrive late having been going round and round on the Underground, completely lost. Or he would be discovered standing in the middle of a sea of traffic while he gazed at architecture from the middle of a city street. He loved things which were beautiful and uncommon. When he left Winchester he took an unusual home made from the gatehouse of Butley Priory in Suffolk. The main buildings have since been demolished. The lichen patinated Gothic stonework reminded him of the College buildings he had left. Staying with him on one occasion, and being undressed and ready for bed, I heard him calling — urgently I thought — 'Wheeler — Wheeler'. When I had hurriedly descended to his room he calmly said: 'Look at these lovely shadows made by my tall traceried windows across my bed. I didn't want you to miss that.' I thought at once of that Rembrandt painting in the National Gallery called *A Scholar in a Lofty Interior* in which moonlight shadows are cast while its studious occupant reads his books. Books and papers were scattered about all over the writing desk at the foot of his bed and on any other available horizontal space.

He thought a modern telephone would be out of place in his living room beneath the high stone-vaulted roof which had for centuries looked down on monks and asses, religious processions, and all the ecclesiastical comings and goings of the ancient Priory. And therefore he had a cubby-hole made to contain it. On the door leading from the great room he had carved in Greek letters not 'Telephone', but 'The Mouth of the Ether'. He kept a table such as became the headmaster of this great Public School and his guests were invited to admire his many beautiful things including plate. I remember at one luncheon a silver cup was passed round 'reputed', the Doctor said, 'to be the work of Benvenuto Cellini'.

We made appropriate noises of appreciation till Kruger Gray who was better informed about such things, gave his unequivocal opinion. 'Not a single Italian feature, all German.' The social barometer fell sharply over the hospitable board.

It was my exceptional good fortune to meet Baker at the tide in my affairs which has led on to what is called 'success'. I was young and comparatively untried when he persuaded the Bank of England rebuilding committee to appoint me as sole sculptor for the rebuilding of their house in the 1920s. This was a commission which any of the established sculptors of the day would have gladly accepted. For this act of faith in me I am ever grateful. It gave me opportunities for sculptural expression which otherwise might never have come my way and for many years secured my livelihood. Standing then on the threshold of my career my mind was full of ideas, my heart eager and my body vigorous, while my hands, through ten years of studentship were trained and capable. This was the young artist's dream. Being very happily and not long married at this time, I was in a seventh heaven. Baker was always encouraging and so was the chairman of the rebuilding committee, Director Booth. George Macaulay Booth with Baker came to my studio to see work in progress very frequently. He too was full of trust, and generous of encouragement. We discussed everything together and together made a team of enthusiasts.

Sir Herbert Baker — he was knighted for his work at Delhi and the Bank — lived in a fine house now tenanted by his eldest son and belonging through his benefaction to the National Trust. I often visited him there, but more frequently we met for breakfast at his house in Smith Square near to his Barton Street office. The routine was to meet in the Victoria Gardens at 7.30, there to pace up and down under the great tower by the river discussing problems of the Arts with special reference to the Bank. Then we went in to his breakfast table to enjoy the delicious kedgeree or other equally nourishing and tasty dishes provided by his faithful Scottish housekeeper, Mrs Donat.

After eating and more talking we separated, I to my studio or the scaffolding and he to his drawing desk both to develop ideas we had been exploring.

I worked with Baker on many another project. One day I will try to count up all the bronzes, stone and wood carvings as well as plaster panels I have made for his buildings. Sufficient idea for the present may be got from the fact that at the Bank alone I sculpted 14 over-life size statues, five large bronze doors 20 feet high, three smaller bronze doors, three busts, a couple of dozen key stones and innumerable bronze handles, medallions, etc., etc.

When Baker was building India House I was wanted there too. The hardest stone I ever carved was Swedish black granite in which I made two lions heads for supporting the balcony over the main door. So hard was the stone that I kept a boy running from studio to smithy so that my chisels could be remade after a dozen or so blows for they then became quite blunt. When South Africa House was being built Baker wanted my work there also, and on the battlefields of France and the playing fields of Winchester my sculpture was erected because Baker believed the arts should be united. He commissioned painters too — Tom Monnington, who was to succeed me as P.R.A., A. K. Lawrence, R.A., Colin Gill and Boris Anrep, who did the mosaic floors in Threadneedle Street, all took their share in making 'The Old Lady' grand. Baker believed in the sisterhood of all the arts and gave a scholarship to the Royal Academy which is awarded in rotation to a sculptor, painter, architect and poet.

Baker was a classicist who saw a great change coming. He thought the engineer would soon usurp many of the architect's functions, that engineering was in the ascendant and architecture in a decline. Had he been living now he would have seen his fears had been well founded. He died in 1946 and was buried in Westminster Abbey. His ashes are interred beneath the nave because the Dean, Bishop de Labillière, told me, he considered him to be 'the great architect of the Commonwealth'. He said to Henry Baker, the eldest son, who went to the Abbey with the sad news: 'We would love to have him here.' Custom required an outside backing. Therefore the Dean asked me if the Academy would present a plea to him for a burial in the Abbey of one of its most distinguished members. To my astonishment the Academy would not do this. When I spoke to Walter Lamb, the Secretary, about it, he received the proposal coldly and muttered something about 'creating a precedent'. This seemed to me to be unreasonable when the initiative had come from the Dean himself.

Lamb's indifference did not damp my ardour though it disappointed me thoroughly. I had rather ashamedly to confess my failure to Dean de Labillière who then asked if I myself would write him a letter and get it signed by half-a-dozen men of importance. This I was able to do. It was necessarily a hasty business. I secured Smuts's signature by cable. Vincent Massey and Lord Salisbury signed willingly, so did Giles Gilbert Scott, but I had difficulty with Munnings, the P.R.A. He reluctantly agreed and then only if Scott would do so. When by appointment I called at Chelsea Park Gardens where he was living, I found him out. By agitated telephoning I eventually reached him, got his consent to sign on his behalf, then raced to the Deanery with the letter, arriving a few minutes before 6 p.m. — zero hour.

Had I needed a spur in this business it would have been provided by a recollection I had of an incident during the war. It was during the first days of the bombing of London. In those days the sound of the sirens sent us all immediately to shelter. (Familiarity with the horror soon altered this.) Baker and I were walking together in Westminster. The warning sounded. He said: 'Shall we go into this shelter or walk on to the Abbey?' He walked on after a moment's pause, saying: 'I'd rather die in the Abbey than in an underground dug-out.'

The Abbey was hit later on as we all know. In the afternoon after the bomb had fallen I met the Dean in Old Palace Yard. He looked ashen and distraught and told me he was taking a short airing after being up all night. Though I protested that he needed to get away from it for a short while, he persisted till I went back with him to the Abbey — for why? 'To see Henry VII's Chapel.

All the glass has gone. The clear light is now streaming in showing all the details of carving and tracery which hasn't been seen before and it looks *so very beautiful.*' It did indeed. How he loved the place and all lovely things.

On another occasion — it was in the Jerusalem Chamber — I recall, he showed me a fine large piece of Persian lapis lazuli which had recently been sent as a present to him. As he turned it round and round in his hands he quoted from Browning's *The Bishop orders His Tomb*:

> *Bedded in store of rotten fig-leaves soft*
> *And carded up in a tight olive-frail*
> *Some lump, ah God, of lapis lazuli*
> *Big as a Jew's head cut off at the nape*
> *Blue as a vein o'er the Madonna's breast.*

He was wondering, he said, how it might be used; in, perhaps, an Altar Cross.

But to return to Baker. Though he enjoyed many friendships, some of them lasting from Lord Milner's kintergarten days, he was not a good 'mixer'. He thought about his work during all his working hours, loved poetry and his garden, particularly a fernery which he tended himself. Without being a prig, he liked the companionship of cultured people. Lawrence of Arabia was one of many. T.E. wrote most of his famous *Seven Pillars of Wisdom* in a top room of No 14, Barton Street, where Baker's office was. A G.L.C. blue plaque now placed on the house says T.E.L. 'lived' there!

It should be remembered that before he came to England from South Africa to build the Bank of England and to co-operate with Lutyens in India, Baker had already made a reputation for 'Baker houses' at the Cape. And then there are what he called the 'five torsos of Cathedrals' at Cape Town, Salisbury, Pretoria, Johannesburg and Nairobi. Groote Schuur, the Cape Town house of the Prime Minister was wholly designed by him from the door knobs to the bath. He told me that he had everything hand-made except the bath and for this he sent to England for the choicest money could buy. Cecil Rhodes, when he saw the completed house expressed himself as being pleased with everything except the bath. When Rhodes had gone back to Pretoria a single block of granite was ordered, hollowed out and placed in the bathroom so that when he came down next time the granite had replaced the enamelled iron. With this Rhodes was delighted, but when one sat down in the bath, however hot the water, one's bottom was always cold, so Baker said.

Cecil Rhodes had presented to the Cabinet Room at Pretoria one of the soapstone Zimbabwe 'birds' hoping, he said, that the wisdom of the ages would preside over the Cabinet's deliberations. So that when Rhodes House was built in Oxford, Baker wanted the same creature as a finial to the dome I made this strange animal in bronze seven feet high. When it was erected, instead of standing vertical as intended, it leaned backwards. Fearing it might be thought to symbolise a drunken Warden, I had a rope put round its neck and got half-a-dozen strong workmen at the other end in South Parks Road to pull with all their might and so bend the anchoring rod and render the 'Zimbabwe' erect and circumspect. While this simple but unusual operation was being carried out under my orders, a quizzical don appeared and said to me in passing, 'What are they doing? Strangling the ugly brute!'

Baker was always grateful to Rhodes and kept on his office mantleshelf a letter Rhodes wrote to his protégé as a young man. This letter told him to go at Rhodes's expense to Athens, Paestum-Agrigentum, Rome and Thebes, to study classical and Egyptian architecture. It was for that reason, I think, that Baker took me — *his* protégé — to Athens, Epidaurus, Corinth, Mycenae and so on to study Greek sculpture, before I began work in Threadneedle Street. It pleased him when an American traveller we met on the boat going to Venice told him that he had said to his wife as they sat at dinner in a hotel at Nauplia where we were the only other guests: 'There goes an English Dean travelling with his two sons ' — one being Alfred an undergraduate at Oxford the other myself.

I remember the delicious butter we were served with. Thinking it was really Arcadian food, we were surprised when, asking for more, it was brought to the table in a tin labelled 'Produce of New Zealand'. At breakfast in Athens next day we imagined the honey came from Hymettus and preferred not to enquire further.

That trip is remembered for very many things. We saw the site of the ancient silver mines at Laurion which was solid scarlet with poppies as they grew after the war on fields of Flanders. I remember the glorious Byzantine mosaics at Daphne in the church with chickens running about in it. It's better cared for now, I'm told. And the roads are better than the dusty one we took to Corinth when we crossed the Peleponesus. Sitting on the steps of the temple there, we shared our lunch with some Greek boys who later stole our knives and forks while we were in the museum. Passing us at Nemæa, where Hercules killed the lion (whose skin he afterwards wore about his loins), went two peasant women looking like carvings from an ancient marble frieze spinning sheep's wool — or was it goat's — from their apron pouches on to their distaffs walking very upright as they descended the hill. Then on to Mycenæ with the famous Lion Gate and afterwards to the tomb of Agamemnon with its colossal lintel surely weighing a hundred tons, over the door. And as the evening was drawing in we sat in the vast theatre at Epidaurus where a whisper from the stage carries to every seat. The spiritis of the great Greek dramatists seemed to be hovering in that elliptical hollow and one felt as one sat there, the place gave one a new insight into Greek drama. I received a similar deeper understanding of Greek sculpture when standing on the Athenian Acropolis. To stand there in that curiously clear light of Greece and look about you gives a more penetrating insight into the sculptures of Myron Phydias, Polyclitus and Praxitiles than do a dozen lectures, however erudite or lucid.

It was in Greece that after visiting Marathon and reflecting upon the Greek wars with the Persians I heard the nightingale for the first time in my life. That was in the pine woods, where many trees had died through gypsies cupping for turpentine, and later that afternoon, sitting on the banks of the shrunken Illysus I remembered Aristophanes while listening to the croaking of the frogs.

Many other unforgettable adventures I had with Baker and I have often thought how different might have been my path if we had not met. I daresay my sculpture, instead of being planned for architecture, would have been designed for galleries and museums. After the first World War 'free' sculpture rapidly grew in popularity and as new forms of architectural expression were developed, sculpture for the adornment of building became less in demand. But I am well content that my sculpture is mostly in the open air on buildings and in public places in company with the milling populace.

Baker was older than I by a generation, but we became great friends. During the unproductive days of the Second World War, and after he had had a stroke, he would struggle down to my studio in Kensington from his office in Westminster, bring his sandwiches, I would make coffee and we would lunch together by a large open wood fire or, in the summer, beneath the old mulberry tree in my garden. He always spoke of art and poetry and often his letters to me would contain his translations from French poets. They concluded with, as signature, a drawing of an old oak tree leaning far over and propped up from falling to the ground. But in those vigorous, productive, 15 years or more before the war, we travelled together in Italy and Greece and all went swimmingly for us in a comparatively stable-seeming world.

It must have been difficult for Baker to leave South Africa where he had done so much pioneer work in the architecture of the new country. But the invitation from Lord Hardinge, the Viceroy of India, to collaborate with Edwin Lutyens in the building of New Delhi proved irresistible. In his book, *Architecture and Personalities*, he refers to the problem which the invitation posed. He wrote: 'I had ... some hesitation and qualms of conscience in the foreknowledge that my acceptance would mean forsaking a trust and allegiance to South Africa, then the happy home of my wife and three sons. [Ann, his daughter, was born later.] South Africa had welcomed and given me of its riches in full measure; and the interests of her art I felt to be a trust imposed upon me by the spirit of Rhodes.'

Baker and Lutyens were old friends taking, when young men, architectural excursions together to study English and Welsh houses. Baker had supported, against local opposition, the name of Lutyens for the design of an Art Gallery in Johannesburg and a monument to men of the Rand Regiment who fell in the Boer War. And although Lutyens was chosen as the chief architect for Delhi, Baker became a willing collaborator. On the strength of his Pretoria Buildings he had been recommended as chief architect for the new capital, but on great pressure from home the Viceroy — (Baker said 'rightly') — appointed Lutyens.

The two 'co-equal' architects worked amicably enough at first. 'Agreement and harmony' prevailed in the settling of the initial plans. They agreed on the site, and that Lutyens should be primarily responsible for Government House and Baker for the Secretariats. They designed together on the boat to and from India in 1913 and then, shortly afterwards, something went wrong and a long lasting animosity arose between them. Baker wrote of it: 'Looking back after many years have passed, I can see more clearly that differences of opinion between myself and Lutyens had their roots in our different natures and outlook on art. I have always held, and still hold, that his intuition and talents in design equalled those of Wren. He concentrated his extraordinary powers and his immense industry and enthusiasm on the abstract and geometrical qualities, to the disregard, I consider, of human and national sentiments and their expression in his art. I, on the other hand, fully realise my inferiority in these talents of the intellect; but content in art, national and human sentiment, and their expression in architecture, seem to me to be of the greatest importance. And this faith grows stronger as my experience grows. It is a quite natural difference in outlook, . . . what more might we not have achieved with unity of counsel.'

The quarrel caused Baker much pain and he very often referred to it in considerable sadness. He was far more generous to Lutyens than he to him, and it was Baker who in their last years made the approach which resulted in a return to a friendship, pale and muted though it was. At least they spoke to each other again. H.B. expressed to me his great concern and sorrow when, on leaving Burlington House one day, President Lutyens had a fall which presaged his demise. Baker always spoke of Lutyens as being a pre-eminent architect and said he 'did things right by instinct'. Lutyens on the other hand often spoke disparagingly of Baker's work and it was Lutyens who blocked for many years H.B.'s election to the Academy. The story goes that when at long last Baker's candidature was successful, as members were leaving the Assembly Derwent Wood, the sculptor, said to Lutyens who was going by: 'You've met your Bakerloo tonight, Lut.' In spite of this, which shows he had no heart in the quarrel, he strongly supported Lutyens candidature for P.R.A.

I do not think Baker's architecture has received the praise which is its due and I am sure that Time will give a truer measure of its merit. He did not have the inclination or aplomb to nip into the limelight. His Union Buildings in Pretoria are a masterpiece and so, in their different way, are the Winchester College War Memorial Cloisters. These are perhaps the loveliest of all the memorials erected by the War Graves Commission after the first world war. The circular Parliament Chamber and Secretariat buildings in Delhi are great works, too. I know that many architects who stood in Lut's penumbra do not share my views and, of course, the young architects of today are anti-classical so cannot be expected to be unbiassed. I think I can truthfully say his work is more appreciated in South Africa by young architects who see how skilfully he chose his sites and worked his design into what he called 'a tapestry'. However, Time will take the full measure of us all.

CHAPTER FIVE

A. R. A.

I SHOULD LIKE to begin this chapter with two extracts from the Press so that I may present a contemporary view of my position and outlook at the time when I was elected an Associate of the Royal Academy. Today is 9th August, 1966, and I quote from this morning's *Times*.

> 'Yet for all his vehemence and sometimes virulent criticism which Sir Charles has received for his orthodoxy, in his younger days he was considered among the leaders of the *avant garde*.'

The second quote was made more than thirty years ago.

> 'The election of Mr Charles Wheeler is a tribute to the advanced school.'

Sir William Llewellyn told me he was at one time considered to be a rebel and yet it was he who in 1934 declared that the Academy was 'lost' if it was going to show work of *my* revolutionary character. And so the Academy marches on and will continue so to do as long as it does not shut its doors on new ideas. This is a conviction I hold strongly and about which I intend to write more in the next chapter.

I was still at work on the Bank of England when I was elected to the Academy. At that time the Italian models who used to sit for us, hearing that an Assembly for Elections was to take place would gather on the steps of Burlington House for the first member to appear outside with the news of who was 'in'. They would then

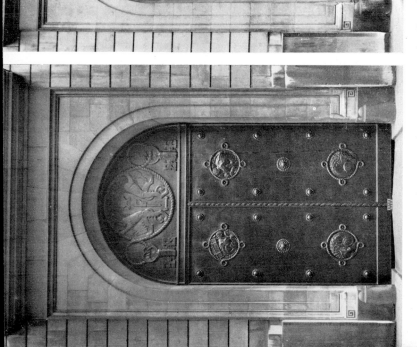

26. Bronze doors: works entrance, Bank of England. 27. Bronze doors; entrance to the bullion yard, Bank of England. 28. Bronze doors: Prince's Street, Bank of England.

29. *Ariel:* sub-treasury dome, Bank of England.

30. *Right and Below*. Bronze door handles at the Bank of England.

31. Montague Norman,
Governor of the Bank of
England: bronze.

32. Lawrence of
Arabia: bronze.

33. India House, Aldwych.

rush away to the fortunate man's studio to acquaint him and to receive the customary guinea. The first arrival received the *pourboir*, but somehow, I suspect, by arrangement — for they were a true fraternity — several appeared together on my doorstep one fine March evening. They were invited in and we all drank something standing looking rather stupid in the middle of the drawing-room till they, having gotten their grateful guineas, took their grinning leave while I was left smiling, I suppose, in smug complacency.

To be elected to the Academy is no small achievement and to me at that juncture in my career it was of the greatest importance. There is no company of Italian models nowadays to run a marathon from Piccadilly to Chelsea or St John's Wood with the good news. It is all done on the 'phone. They have gone, to my regret, for they were a colourful piece in the studio tapestry up to 1939. They could be relied upon to turn up for sittings. To sit well was professional craftsmanship in which they took great pride. Their bodies were mostly well made, golden coloured, with a stolid Latin cast of anatomy. Where now are the Mancinis Domenico, Gulio, Antonio and the rest? Grandfather, sons and grandsons all of whom served so well the artists of the nineties and the first forty years of this century. They lived frugally and saved every penny, sold hot potatoes on winter evenings when they had no sittings and, in the summer, ice cream in Hammersmith and Shepherds Bush. It was not uncommon, I am told, for them to return with their savings after many years of hard work, to their native villages and become the mayor of the place.

But I digress. I was now a member of that great institution founded by Sir Joshua Reynolds from whose schools came Turner, Constable and Flaxman and whose membership has included so many other great names: Chambers, Benjamen West, Millais and Augustus John. I was very proud, have worn the pride on my sleeve ever since and, for the past ten years, the Presidential badge about my neck.

I was at once appointed to the Selection Committee for the

Annual Summer Exhibition and began to realise how democratic and just were its dealings, how surely based it is upon the principles designed by the founders and approved by King George III. In the succeeding years I have come to regard the Academy with increasing admiration and affection. It is apparent to me that this independent body of artists elected *by* artists who govern a two hundred year old Academy and make it pay its own way, is more necessary in the art world of today than ever it was in the days of its undisputed rule in the nineteenth century. Here is a free art school, here is a free company of painters, sculptors and architects. As a body they are not to be dictated to by government officials nor dealers. We are not subjected to pressure groups; critics or the irregularities of the art market dealings and we choose works for our annual exhibitions not because they have a potential $33\frac{1}{3}\%$ commission on sales for us, but simply because we think they are good examples. When works of art have become dangerously near being merely commercial commodities, then an Academy which is unaffected by such consideration maintains a corrective to this unhealthy tendency.

Sir William Llewellyn was P.R.A. when I joined. He was admirably circumspect, looked the part and reigned undisputed ruler of our affairs. We all stood up when he entered. His successor, Sir Edwin Lutyens, was a man of very different mould, brilliant as an architect, hopeless as a Chairman. During the business of his first council meeting he made funny sketches on a note pad he always kept in his pocket. He passed one over to me much to the frowning displeasure of Walter Lamb, the Lewellyn-circumspect secretary. The sketch was folded in a cunning way so that the drawn man standing by a stile appeared to jump over the stile when the ends were pulled apart. When he saw my surprise he roared with laughter, a very unseemly conduct for a P.R.A. so Lamb thought. But Lut was full of fun, irrepressible in his joking, all designed I think as a clown's mask, to hide the serious countenance of his true genius. The stories of his fun are legion as the excellence of his numerous buildings is undoubted. His was a muted presidential term because of the war years 1940–44. When he died in office a great funeral service for him was held at Westminster Abbey, the cortège starting from Burlington House — passing the Cenotaph in Whitehall on the way to Parliament Square. Sir Herbert Baker, Sir Henry Rushbury and I rode in one carriage together and, as Rushbury has reminded me since, (I confess I do not remember it at all), when we left the Academy Baker turned to me and said: 'Charles, you must be President one day'.

When a new leader was to be chosen two rival camps developed. There were followers of Augustus John and supporters of Alfred Munnings, both picturesque characters. The latter was eventually top of the poll because, so I believe, the majority thought John would not stand up so well to the routine of the office. Munnings was intolerant of new ideas and perhaps a too outspoken critic of experiment and modernism. He was the first P.R.A. who had to face the full force of violent charges, floods of 'isms' and blusters of gimmicks.

Now was a turning point in Academy affairs and he fought a rearguard action against the experimenters. With what energy did he battle, this devoted champion of true art as he saw it! It led him into contests which he did not always win with many artists and critics who were equally committed to other causes. He had many a tilt at John Rothenstein, then Director of the Tate Gallery, who, he said, was filling the gallery with rubbish. A.J., as we all called him, was not a tolerant man. He felt too strongly about art. So strong were his views that he couldn't imagine why others could possibly have different opinions and this often caused rowdy scenes at the lunch table and committee meetings, but they usually ended amicably enough and he bore little malice.

He was an unusual man and knew by memory page upon page of Surtees, and long quotations from Shakespeare; these together with his own rhymes he would regale us with over the port at dinner. His choice was eclectic and would be marked at times by sharp and sudden contrasts. I remember him, on one occasion, quoting some bawdy verses he had written at the Café Royal in its famous days before the first World War, when it was patronised by the bohemian artistic set including Augustus John, Roger Fry, Walter Sickert and many others. When someone protested they had had enough he switched at once to *The Rape of Lucrece* ... 'Time's glory is to calm contending kings, To unmask falsehood and bring truth to light, To stamp the seal of time in aged things, To wake the morn and sentinel the night, ...' The effect was electric. His memory was truly remarkable and his brain as incisive as his pencil and as sweeping as his brush.

At the Academy we have a dining club which meets three or four times a year and these occasions provided Munnings, when in the Chair and in the mood, with the opportunity to keep the company long at the table while he held forth on art and horses or books, and encouraged others to do the same. This made many a memorable evening. A. K. Lawrence, R.A. also had the capacity to memorise and I recall how he declaimed in a histrionic manner and with his very powerful voice from *The Tempest*. A.K. was especially fond of this play and of Caliban's speech beginning 'The isle is full of noises, music and soft airs that give delight and hurt not....'.

A.J.'s championship of long established standards led him to war against the *avant garde* and brought him and the Academy much publicity. The buried bulk of the Chantrey Collection he persuaded the Tate Gallery Trustees to unearth so that they could be shown at Burlington House for one of the Winter Exhibitions, which to their surprise was so great a success that at the close of the exhibition A.J. with the consent of his Council sent the works back together with a cheque for £1,000 towards their then very scanty purchase funds. The notorious Banquet Speech in which he made very disparaging remarks on Picasso and his art brought a storm of abuse about his unbending head from the leaders and followers of the new art forms which Pablo practised. It offended the French Ambassador who was one of the distinguished guests, delighted the popular press and brought both praise and acrimony to the door of Burlington House. His letters always had the special impress of his unique personality as the following one, written in the summer of 1956, when he was championing my candidature for presidency will show:

'Dear Charles. In case I don't get you on the 'phone (as I leave for Newmarket each morning) will you and your mate and daughter meet us at the Forum Club at 7 o'clock on Thursday evening. The great VIOLET — the almighty woman — will be there, as she prances or strolls and gorges at the Garden Party at the Palace that afternoon — whilst I listen to the sky lark's songs on Newmarket Heath — see 'osses and jockeys at the Starts and lie at length on the grass in between the races away from the horror of the Metropolis.

'So you be there, Charles, if not completely worn out chipping a round bottom of some female or nymph with dolphin — or an Aphrodite — not like that bloody thing in ... gardens!!

'Yours, Alfred M'.

Munnings retired at the age of 70 saying he was tired. Afterwards he seemed to lose his wonted zest. He was more content to tread softly — though he would sometimes still stamp like Pegasus or Helicon when disturbed by some 'modern atrocity'.

Gerald Kelly, a colourful character from an Irish mould, was elected to succeed A.J. and for the following five years ruled us with extraordinary vigour and frequent rudeness. On the evening of his election he said to me: 'You know, Wheeler, I've spent my life being rude to people, now I shall have to change.' 'You won't,' I replied. Neither did he. His Irish temperament led him into disputing with Humphrey Brooke, the Secretary of the Royal Academy, and with the membership in Council meetings and General Assemblies, but he worked like a Trojan for the good of the Academy. He produced a series of Winter Exhibitions of old masters which brought honour and glory, as well as financial success, to the institution and caused him to find a place for himself as a most popular television broadcaster. His broadcasts had a wide appeal by their racy nature, and by an infectious delight in the craft of the painter, they resulted in a phenomenal swelling in attendances to exhibitions. The occasional indiscretion of a swear word inserted in the most 'telling' place gave that piquancy for an uncultivated appetite which appealed to a section of the public unused to art appreciation and they responded by coming to the Academy in their thousands. The Kelly presidency will always be highly regarded in Academy history. He was so vigorous at 75 that one felt inclined to doubt the wisdom of our age limit, for I think he could have gone on for another five with undiminished ardour.

Originally, of course, P.R.A.s could remain in office till they died. Sir Joshua Reynolds served in the Chair for 24 years, to be followed by Benjamen West, the American-born President, who had 28 years and thirdly Sir Thomas Lawrence, ten years. In recent times members have been elected at riper years, but, in spite of that, there have been only 18 holders of the first office of the Academy since its foundation in 1768.

The seventeenth P.R.A. was Sir Albert Richardson, the architect, elected when he was 74, but who, by Royal Assent, remained in office till 76. He organised a fine exhibition of Portuguese Art in the Winter of 1953–54, which revealed a national style of which we in England then knew very little. Apart from this there is not much to record of his two years. 'Albert Edward', like his two precursers, was a colourful person. Just as Munnings dug his feet in about painting Richardson did likewise about architecture and he was just as indiscreetly outspoken, but he had a clever wit. Architecture at the time was altering just as violently as were the other arts, but A.E. kept an even course. He stood firm upon the classical shore, letting the mighty waves of revolutionary ideas beat about him. He would only shake his brine-soaked head and look defiant. One of his great hates was the concrete lamp-post for his architectural light burnt atop an eighteenth-century silver candelabrum with an eighteenth century clarity and grace. He surrounded himself — nay, hemmed himself in rather — with things of beauty. His Georgian house at Ampthill was loaded with pictures, period furniture and *objets d'art*. At public dinners I have seen him bring out from his white waistcoat pocket a small silver paint box, dip a sable brush in his glass and make a wine-colour drawing of the scene about him, then present it to the Lord Mayor.

He had a remarkable facility with his pencil and I recall one special occasion which showed this in convincing fashion. A City Company wished to refurbish their Court Room and he and I were asked to lunch there. The Professor asked for a board and easel with charcoal to be placed in the room so that after the meal he could demonstrate what he proposed. Working to a large scale he sketched before their amazed eyes their somewhat dowdy hall and then with a few deft strokes he put a curtain here, windows and mirrors there, a crystal chandalier depending from the ceiling and rubbing out several ugly features, transformed their ordinary room into a palatial salon. The money for it, which it had been feared might be difficult to get, then flowed freely!

'Albert Edward' was a brilliant lecturer and loved talking to students. He was Bartlett Professor at London University for many years and Professor of Architecture at the Academy too. On coming down the Burlington House staircase with him one day, he said to me: 'My boy, I'm 70 today. I'm going to talk to students. I talked to them when I was seventeen and I shall go on talking to them till I die.' He used to make his own lantern slides by brilliantly drawing diagrams in ink on glass. He would invite the R.A. Schools students down to his place at Ampthill and after entertaining them with talk, showing them his treasures and giving them tea, would dress up in eighteenth-century costume and wave them off standing clad in velvet surcoat and breeches on his doorsteps.

After his fashion he loved the Academy well and I was glad that such a champion of the beautiful as he should be the one to take the presidential chain from his shoulders and put it upon mine.

CHAPTER SIX

P. R. A.

THE PRESIDENT of the Royal Academy is elected annually around about 10th December — 'Founders' Day'. Until he reaches the normal retiring age of all Academicians — 75 — his re-election is understood to be more or less of a formality. When a new P.R.A. is to be chosen a large attendance at the Assembly is assured. After the statutory and sometimes long-drawn-out process of balloting has brought a result the members are 'locked in' and although no white smoke is emitted from Burlington House chimney, the approval of our 'Patron, Protector and Supporter' the Sovereign is sought by telephone to Buckingham Palace, before the doors are 'unlocked' and the result can be made known to the Press.

In 1956 there were three holders of the high office present and after my election the four of us were photographed together. I wonder if so many will ever be shown together again. The quartet consisted of Munnings, Kelly, Richardson and myself.

Thus I found myself, the eighteenth P.R.A. and the first sculptor to be chosen. As is customary, members dined together that evening and I was placed sitting opposite our great marble sculpture Michelangelo's Tondo of the *Virgin and Child with St John* and I thought of the Fifteenth Discourse of the first P.R.A., Sir Joshua Reynolds. It will be remembered that the closing words of that lecture ran: 'I feel a self-congratulation in knowing I am capable of those sensations he intended to excite. I reflect not without vanity that these Discourses bear testimony of my admiration for that truly divine man, and I should desire that the last words I should pronounce in this Academy and from this place, might be the name of Michelangelo.' After that he never spoke more in the Academy. With these words in mind and that wonderful work of art looking me in the face I was abashed and devoid of appetite. Since that first evening in the Assembly Room I have presided over many meetings there, where important decisions have been taken regarding our Schools, exhibitions and the general functioning of our institution. As President I have entertained at that table the important, learned, great, gracious and lovely of this land and from overseas, but have never looked up at that masterpiece without being thrilled and humbled. I have asked that my chair shall always be placed opposite it. As my tenure of office is drawing to a close the marble has been moved from Burlington House to be shown elsewhere and when it returns to us may well occupy another place in the building. But I am happy to remember that its 'presence' has permeated the Assembly Room throughout the whole of my presidency.

It is an undoubted honour to be the P.R.A., but how was I to continue with my sculpture? A great number of large works were on the stocks at the time of my election, and I had to run the Academy from the top. This was my problem. The solution on which I resolved was that I must organise my studio work by more careful planning — I must make more decisions on first thoughts (second are not always best) and must fill the mornings with concentrated activity in my studio, leaving the afternoons and evenings open and ready if needed for Academy duties. This scheme could not have succeeded had I not been fortunate in having two lieutenants of the first calibre. As a sculptor I had my devoted assistant Chadwick, as the P.R.A. there was Humphrey Brooke, the Secretary of rare ability. To both these men I am indebted more than I can tell for without them I could not have got through the most concentrated decade of my life comparatively unscathed. During the ten years the business of the Academy has I believe never been heavier or, because of art's capricious behaviour, more difficult and the same applies to the problems of my sculptural practice. Of my works and of these two men I shall be writing in succeeding chapters.

As I conceived it, it was my duty as President to carry on the established traditions of the Academy, but also to mould it to new conditions for it was now the middle of the twentieth century when eighteenth- and nineteenth-century outlooks were no longer solely current. If then there had been complacency there was now no room for it. I was convinced that the Academy should open its doors more widely than had been necessary or possible under my predecessors. This was not an easy persuasion for a lover of tradition to arrive at and I remembered G. K. Chesterton's 'Tradition is the democracy of the dead. Tradition refuses to submit to the small and arrogant oligarchy of those who merely happen to be walking around.' But, after all, the war had changed approaches to and outlooks on so many things including the Arts, and what was good enough for the Victorians was not unquestionably good for Elizabethan experimental artists living in an atomic and space-exploration age.

I decided, therefore, that I would do what I could to encourage the showing in our galleries of works of all persuasions as long as they were good examples of their kind. I personally thought many of them were like a rash on a fevered patient and I believed that by letting it come out a healthier state would follow. But as leader of a great cultural institution, such thinking apart, I was intent upon a policy of tolerance on a wide front. I meant to attach particular importance to the rigorous protection of freedom of expression though I might hate its form.

Now this has its dangers and it was not what Munnings, who did so much lobbying for my candidature, expected. It has often plunged me into the rough waters between the Scylla whirlpool of modernism and eddies of the Charybdis of tradition. Whether my approach to the dilemma was right or wrong others must decide, but I am not persuaded that, should it be possible for Sir Joshua to leave his pedestal in the courtyard of Burlington House and pass through the turnstiles to see the current 1966 Summer

Exhibition, he would entirely disapprove of the attempted solution of a problem it was not his misfortune to have to wrestle with. Though I am certain he would have been as sad as I am.

Being a member of the Hanging Committee a little while before I became President, I placed in the Exhibition a certain piece of sculpture which I thought was good. Munnings was P.R.A. at the time and in a particularly vociferous outburst demanded its removal. When I refused to co-operate he stormed out of the galleries at a great speed until the echoes of his threats of resignation died away in the distance. But of course he didn't resign. I have never known why, after that incident, he thrust me forward as candidate when Richardson finished. He never asked me what my policy would be nor did he discuss art with me at all. Dictation not discussion was his cue at all times. Artists are people holding very firm opinions — a fine thing in their creative sphere — but they spill over at times and that spirit of compromise which is essential to the proper running of such a democratic institution as ours is often hard to generate. Therefore this sort of thing happens in the Academy sometimes. But in general I have had the loyal support of the majority of my R.A. and A.R.A. colleagues.

I have tried to make the Academy into a microcosm of a sensible world wherein individuality is not diluted or compounded and wherein credit should be given for qualities we may not like and do not ourselves possess, where tolerance and trust are considered to be better than mistrust, where freedom of thought is admitted and no genuine expression is stifled, wherein we should try to think that our particular God of Beauty (so long as it is a god and not a puppet) is not the only one, nor that truth in art has but one facet merely. Of course it is inevitable that in the free and generous exercise of tolerance and trust one gets taken in sometimes by charlatanry, but I have always regarded that as being better than an arthritic bigotry at all times. Not in art alone, of course, do we have to judge between the true and the false. We cannot escape the responsibility in so many walks of life.

During the last ten years some very strange works have hung on the walls and stood in the sculpture galleries, forms of art which would have been unthinkable only a few years ago, works which have given me personally no pleasure at all — displeasure rather — but such is the democratic basis of our structure and so firmly held my conviction about tolerance in our world of change that I consider it vital to the well-being of the Academy to admit all works of free expression which seem to some of us to have merit. For this reason is the Royal Academy — an independent body — so important in this day and age. Under its aegis is an island of freedom. It is only by being untramelled that the cleft and distorted world of art can find its way back to a more wholesome future. I have not found it easy to fulfil two roles. As a sculptor I should be hopeless without principles of art which I hold with absolute conviction. At Burlington House I have frequently been obliged to give credit, but like Robert Browning to Baldasaro 'with such a heavy mind'. At the Academy the President has had to recognise the claims and opinions of many egotists (all artists are egotists — if not they could not be artists) and at Cathcart Road but one — himself. He has often felt his two-self personality torn to shreds in the change-over from one to the other.

Reynolds's Academy in its long history has never been free from detractors and can list among them William Blake and Charles Dickens, but exposure to the elements of rough criticism has helped in the strengthening of its constitution. Likewise it has always had friends. Would that I could boast that during my term of office the sum of detractors had dwindled, but I fear I cannot. I hope I may justly think that we have no fewer friends than when I took up the reins.

In my numerous contacts wherever I have been whether in the provinces, in the metropolis, whether in America, Europe or Australasia I have been proud to hear good things said of us. One would think the art-boys and the majority of laymen were speaking of different bodies when each make reference to us.

Artists are romantically supposed to be bad businessmen, but only artists have governed the Academy since it was founded by the Sovereign in 1768, and — this is the fact which surprises so many — we have remained the whole while solvent and independent. Our non-fee-paying schools have been maintained unaided, we have mounted great exhibitions and administered numerous Trust Funds. For the welfare of the Arts we have laboured without cease. This record has been made possible through our own earnings and we have therefore been unhindered by controls except those self-imposed. This is how it should be with artists.

If, through my presidency, a continuance of that freedom for the forseeable future is made more possible I shall be glad and grateful. At what cost this may have been secured the story will be told if you, my readers, continue turning these pages.

The presidential duties require the attendance at many social functions, the opening of many exhibitions and the making of numerous speeches, the words of which must be weighed carefully. At the end of a day's modelling or carving, it is hard going to be obliged to get into dress clothes and meet fresh people. But new contacts have proved stimulating and I have gone to bed afterwards and, on the whole, slept well. It has been my great good fortune to have my lovely wife to help me in these duties. She has always dressed beautifully in clothes of her own designing and has never once complained though she must have found the effort much harder than I. Everyone has loved her wherever we have gone. She gets on better with strangers than I. Her success is due to a sweet simplicity and childlike belief in the fundamental goodness of humanity together with an innate championship of the under dog. Her father once told me he thought she would hold a brief for the Devil, who, I suppose, might be considered to be something of an under dog! One of the functions she could not attend was the Annual Dinner because, until November 1966, we had always kept it a strictly male gathering, but she has received with me many thousands of guests standing with me at the top of the great staircase at Burlington House, and I have always been mightily proud of her.

At the annual dinners, people of great importance assemble, Archbishops, Dukes, Ambassadors, Prime Ministers, chiefs of the Services, leaders of learning and industry, scientists, poets, artists and so on. I have presided at ten of them, and at seven have had sitting next to me our Honorary Royal Academician Extraordinary, Sir Winston Churchill; he always enjoyed these functions, so Lady Churchill told us.

I recall how his election came about. It was during the presidency of Sir Alfred Munnings and one evening when we were gathered together he was urging us to elect the great man to membership. There would be no chance, of course, of his election in the ordinary way. 'Couldn't he be an honorary member?', A. J. asked of Walter Lamb, who replied that under our Laws honorary members had to be foreign artists of great distinction and we had no class of membership into which W.S.C. could fit. When I suggested — and I take credit for this — 'Honorary Royal Academician Extraordinary' it seemed apt and fitting. So, with the approval of the Monarch, the matter was agreed.

As a measure of his ability as an artist let me record that in 1947 he submitted two paintings to the Academy Summer Exhibition under the name of 'David Winter'. They were both passed by the Selection Committee and hung on the walls before the identity of the author was known. One of these is now in the Tate Gallery's Collection. Augustus John in a letter to me about Churchill wrote: 'Like everybody I am staggered by his adventures with painting which he tackles with the same gusto and fearlessness we have learned to expect of his other activities. This never fails him.'

Before sending-in day for the Summer Exhibition Sir Winston would ask me to help him choose his paintings. I remember that year when I went to No 28, Hyde Park Gate for this purpose. Mr Montague Browne received me and asked me if I would go to Sir Winston's bedroom as the doctor wanted him to rest that day. On the stairs I met Lord Moran coming down. 'Shall I tire the patient if I talk art to him?' I asked. 'Talk about his pictures', he replied, 'it will do him good.' On entering his room I found him sitting up in bed with a bed table across his knees on which there were writing materials and he was smoking a cigar. The time was 11 a.m. and I was at once invited to have a cigar and a whisky with him. By his side was a cage with his budgerigar, Toby, and on the right side of his bed a large picture of the Houses of Parliament. This 'House of Commons man' would naturally open his eyes first thing each day on this painting. In a large arc around the room were placed a number of his canvases and as I sat by his bedside, he on my right — I on his left with the pet bird between, we discussed the merits of each in turn and he would tell me of when, where and how it was painted. All this with obvious pleasure.

Meanwhile Toby was released, flew about the room and then perched on my hand while I was making notes. Toby was allowed much freedom. I have seen him at the luncheon table perch on the edges of coffee cups and very nearly upset them. My daughter learned from his secretary that when they went abroad arrangements for the pet bird were far more difficult to make than all the others. That visit was indeed a memorable one. There was one of the greatest men of all time whose leadership had saved us from the most terrible disasters which had ever threatened any people, one who had stood defiant upon the highest human hill, against fearsome odds, lying relaxed in bed surrounded by things which give ordinary men pleasure and simple people delight.

On another occasion Lady Churchill being indisposed, Sir Winston and I lunched alone together at Hyde Park Gate, driving afterwards to Chartwell. At a road crossing in Streatham the car pulled up for the lights where a small crowd of shoppers were waiting to cross. When they saw their national hero, they waved and cheered. He was patently pleased and turning to me said: 'They're very civil, aren't they?' A Churchillian choice of a word, I thought. When we arrived at his house I noticed a decoration rather prominently displayed in the drawing room. I enquired what it was and he replied: 'Oh, that's the Croix de Liberation that was given to me by General de Gaulle. It has been given to only three people — President Roosevelt, myself and the Sultan of Morocco. I am going to Marrakesh next week and so shall be seeing my "buddy".'

Muriel, Carol my daughter and I one early spring day in 1960 went to Chartwell to see his studio and to choose a Diploma Picture he was to give to the Academy. As we sat together in comfortable chairs he in the middle we on either side while picture after picture was brought down (there were 350 of them placed close together on the walls) and put upon an easel before us. We chose a painting of Avignon.

When we went up to the house for luncheon, Lady Churchill pretending to be cross, said: 'Do you know what you have done, Winston? You've given away the picture you gave me as a birthday present.' I said at once, of course, that we could choose another, but she told me she wanted him to be represented by the best and if I had chosen *Avignon* we should have it.

The very next morning I received a letter from Sir Winston in which he wrote: 'I am greatly complimented that you should wish to have one of my pictures for the Diploma Room. I feel rather reluctant, however, to take *Avignon* away from Lady Churchill. I gave it to her some time ago and she is fond of it. I wonder if you would like to have the other one which you were looking at, the one of sea and rocks and trees at Cap d'Ail which you found was characteristic of my painting? I should be delighted if you cared to have this. But if you would prefer to reflect further on the matter, perhaps we could leave it until I return to England in April. With all good wishes,

'Yours v. sincerely,
W.S.C.'

Several times afterwards I viewed his paintings with him at Hyde Park Gate. He was latterly dressed in a deep blue velvet suit — the blue of the garter mantle. The house was always full of flowers and to me, as President of the Academy to which he belonged and for which he had a high regard and warm affection,

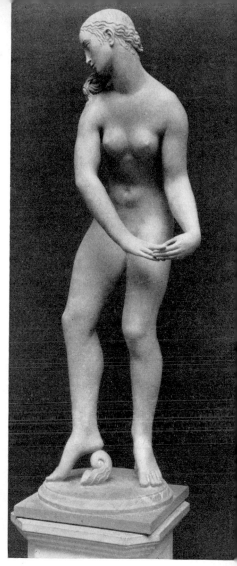

34. *Nymph of the Rippling Waters:* statue
exhibited in the R.A. (1938).

35. Artist's wife: gilt bronze
(1937).

36. 'Zimbabwe' bird: Rhodes
House, Oxford.

37. *Right*. Winged springbok:
gilt bronze on South Africa
House.

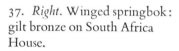

38. Pelican: St John's College,
Johannesburg.

39. Lord Hives: chairman of Rolls Royce Ltd.

JELLICOE
1859-1935

40. Admiral Jellicoe in Trafalgar Square.

41. Mermaid Group: Trafalgar Square.

42. Triton group: Jellicoe memorial fountain, Trafalgar Square.

he was always warm and courteous. After one of my Banquet speeches he turned and, touching my hand, said, 'Well done'. If it were possible, though I very much doubt it, I would that posterity could of my term of office, echo that sentiment.

CHAPTER SEVEN

THE SALE OF THE
• CARTOON

DURING THE LONG lifetime of the Academy, though it has collected many works of art, collecting has never been one of its major concerns. Instruction in its schools, the promotion of the Fine Arts through exhibitions and the administration of many Trust Funds have been the three chief activities of the Institution since it was founded in 1768. Among the treasures which have come to us by purchase or gift there are two which in value and importance stand head and shoulders above the rest. The Carrara marble Tondo by Michelangelo and the Leonardo da Vinci Cartoon of the Virgin and Child with St Anne and St John. The Tondo came to us through the will of Sir George Beaumont in 1830, but it is not known how we acquired the Cartoon. We *do* know that within the twelfth year of our foundation it was hanging in the Drawing School when Somerset House was our home. A drawing, very recently discovered, by Edward Burney (a cousin of the famous Fanny), who was an R.A. student of the school, shows this clearly.

When I became P.R.A. in 1956 the Academy's financial affairs had already given some of us cause for concern and in the following few years it became increasingly difficult for us to pay our way. I must here explain that except for dippings into the Privy Purse during our first 12 years or so, to the extent of £5,000 which the King graciously and generously allowed us to do, and for a grant of £6,000 from the Pilgrim Trust during the second World War, the Academy has always paid its own way. It has never sought other help or taken grants from any source whatsoever. Bad businessmen as artists are romantically supposed to be, the members of the Royal Academy have succeeded in always paddling their own canoe. They have done it by carefully building up a capital fund, through the holding of exhibitions in the past and by continuing to hold them summer by summer and winter by winter up to the present time. We are a little proud of having done this which has as a consequence allowed us to be absolutely independent.

The tumbling down of the value of the pound in this century, especially since the second World War, caused a crisis in the Academy's affairs and it became clear to us that some drastic action must be taken. I shall never forget the day in January, 1962 (after the bad start to the *Primitives to Picasso* Exhibition) when I had an earnest private talk with Humphrey Brooke, the Academy Secretary, about our budget. Things looked black; we had clearly reached an impasse. How were we to go forward? There were two ways only. One was to beg for help, the other was to help ourselves. The former would mean a degree of loss of independence. The other would lead to a continuance of unimpared independence. At what level of importance did we place the independence we had kept from our foundation? It was surely at the highest. Freedom from outside interference is essential to an artist. To the Academy, in these days particularly, its freedom from obligations to anyone but itself is an asset to be preserved above all else. Of this, more later. In this conviction Humphrey and I were instantly and jointly certain and almost together we said: 'We must sell the Leonardo Cartoon.' We knew this to be a possession of great value, but Oh! why must we choose between the two? I recall the hollow silence that followed during which we realised what a dreadful thing we had said. It was like a great betrayal. This supreme masterpiece had looked down on the affairs of our house with its Leonardo smile for nearly 200 years. It was a benign presence giving us daily its benediction of beauty.

Whenever we went into the room it was always there, the same, the changeless, and it never let us down; it pervaded the place and now we had, like traitors, thought to banish the presence — and after such faithfulness! 'Let us go and see it,' we said, again almost together. We passed through the Saloon and in to the Council Room and were met by *the smile* which we could not return and from which we quickly turned away. It could not be endured.

This was the sorrowful beginning; we suffered agonies before the ending. Events had to move quickly. A Special Council meeting was summoned and to my great relief the members accepted the explanation of the need for action and the course proposed. Quickly again a General Assembly was summoned, for this was a major act. With considerable trepidation I faced a large gathering of my colleagues who knew we were to discuss an important matter, but of what importance and of what nature they were totally ignorant.

As I rose from the Chair I can recall there was a great hush and I felt very, very much alone. I am not sure but I like to think I was calm enough to explain clearly the dire situation in which we found ourselves and the painful remedy which was proposed to redress it. When I sat down I felt as a prisoner might do in the dock waiting for his sentence. The few moments seemed like an age. The hush ended — approval came, the Assembly splendidly backed up the decision we had made and with only one dissentient we now had authority to sell one of the two High Renaissance treasures we possessed and one of the greatest works of art in the world. It was the unanimous wish of our members that when sold it should remain in this country. My own opinion was not adamant on this point.

We had already planned the next steps. Again speed and secrecy were essential because we knew that when news of the sale was announced, we should be beseiged by the Press. It is not always so, but on this occasion the members kept a marvellous confidence. We were so grateful for this, because the next thing was to offer the first refusal to the Government. The Council thought this patriotic and right, and so did the membership.

Meanwhile, we had obtained independently from three of the leading art dealers an estimation of the figure the Cartoon would be likely to fetch in the saleroom. The average arrived at was £750,000. We thereupon offered it to the government for £675,000. All through these initial moves we had the experience and advice, freely given, of that great friend of the Academy, Lord Pearce.

After some little time during which we thought the National Gallery was being consulted, the surprising reply came that the that as far as they were concerned the Cartoon might well go out of the country. This was confirmed at a meeting Brooke and I had with the First Secretary of the Treasury and other government officials. It was the policy of the government, we were told, to interfere as little as possible with the free trading in works-of-art and that, if at the subsequent sale, it should be bought by someone from America or Italy or elsewhere, they did not see why an export licence should not, after the usual delay of six months or so, be granted. There was no certain guarantee of this from that source however. This was worrying, because if the masterpiece could be sold without fear of an export licence being witheld, the bidding was naturally likely to be higher than otherwise.

Nevertheless, we commissioned Messrs Sotheby's to undertake the complicated business of the selling of this most famous Leonardo. With this the news was out. The Press, as we guessed, seized on it and we were commended in 95–100% of the news-papers for our declared intention to pay our own way. *The Times* of 10th March, 1962, in a leader urging the need to secure the work for the Nation and entitled 'Everybody's Business' wrote: 'The Academicians have shown proud courage in deciding to sell their Leonardo da Vinci masterpiece. So great will be the shock of this morning's announcement, so hurtful to national dignity the state of necessity in a world-famous British institution thus revealed, that the instinctive reaction will be to challenge this view. Those who force the public to face painful facts are seldom praised. . . .

'There will be an immediate demand that the work shall stay in the United Kingdom. This will be right. It has become almost a cliché that Britain must painfully adjust herself to her altered circumstances and both wisely and effectively find her new place in the world. The nation has not yet reached the pass, however, when it can no longer afford to keep one of its greatest artistic treasures. If the Leonardo goes abroad it will not be for lack of money but for lack of spirit. . . . The issue goes beyond the masterpiece. It is whether the British people will register their new place among the nations by showing that altered circumstances have not destroyed old values, that having it individually good includes preserving the national treasures of the mind and hand and spirit. Let them do this and the noise of it will go round the world.'

As I have already said the members of the Academy were, from the first, unanimous in their wish that the work should stay within these shores and were willing to sacrifice money if that would secure its retention here. While I supported this view as P.R.A., I was conscious throughout that, so great was this masterpiece, that it truly belongs to humanity and we at the Academy had only been the privileged custodians of it for a fifth of a millenium. It was perhaps unwise of me to let this personal opinion have prominence in my Banquet speech because that may have been a contributing cause for the Press abuse which mounted up later. No one really likes reflections made on what *The Times* called 'lack of spirit.' Noticing the slow progress of the National Appeal I had said: 'The question is prompted "Does Britain deserve to retain the Cartoon?" If it does its people will not hold back any longer. If it does not . . . then let it go to America or where you will if there there is a livelier care for beauty and a less unpolished pride in things of the mind.'

Front page headlines appeared in the world Press. The general approval we had received brought us relief after weeks of great anxiety, but this was only a lull before the storm. There was great national concern about the possibility of a foreign buyer coming and taking the cartoon away with him. This agitation stirred the Government from apathy and I then received a letter from the Prime Minister asking if I would recommend to the R.A. Assembly a postponement of the sale in order that a country-wide appeal could be made by the National Arts Collection Fund. This meant calling another meeting of Academicians. It was hurriedly convened and we decided to do as the Prime Minister requested.

After the news had first been given the estimated value of the Cartoon grew and grew, the figure of one million was the round figure at this time.

A delay of the sale for three months was agreed so that £800,000 could be raised. Messrs Sotheby's were splendid about this and took no fee of any kind. This reduction troubled me then and has done so since, but my colleagues argued that if we could not fix the price at £675,000 (our original offer), we should make some discount from the new estimate. As the senior Academy Trustee I was unhappy about offering one of our assets for sale so much below its market value and it troubles me to this day. I fear we shall one day be blamed by our successors. But after pressing for £900,000 I squared my conscience with the argument advanced by our legal Counsel that with the £200,000 reduction we should purchase public esteem and national gratitude. How fallacious this was. The N.A.C.F. got busy, but were fractious about the increase from £675,000 to £800,000. The first figure was given to the government in strict confidence and we have no reason to suppose that they ever disclosed it, but someone did. The difference in our offers seemed to trigger off a barrage of abuse and from where we had had previously received praise we got denigration. The attitude of the Press changed over-night and I was conscious that the Academy had enemies who spread falsities about us. Lie followed lie. We were accused of many things, including giving too little time to raise the money. This last point was, to our amazement, raised by the Chairman of the Fund himself. We reminded him that in a letter immediately after we told him he could go ahead he said he considered our time allocation 'just right' and that too much time would be harmful as it would dispel the sense of urgency he thought to be necessary.

Questions and answers in Parliament piled on the criticism, and added to the list of prevarications. In a television interview with Richard Crossman I faced blatant abuse and distortions which harassed and distressed me. Roy Jenkins came to see me for the press; his report showed the general Fleet Street bias. Only a few days before I had received a letter from David Crawford in which he expressed his gratitude to the R.A. for making the Appeal possible. He spoke of the difficulties his committee were about to encounter and added: 'Good luck to us all. At least your anxieties are over. . . .' How mistaken he was!

Day after day for weeks on end one accusing finger after another was pointed at us. 'We had no right to sell.' 'We were blackmailing the British Public.' 'We were avaricious.' 'We stood for worthless art and were no longer capable of fulfilling our fundamental purpose, namely to provide sound technical teaching in the various artistic media.' This last is how Douglas Cooper put it in a bitter attack in the *Sunday Telegraph* of 22nd July. He enlarged his spleen by adding: 'No intelligent person would deny that such a supreme work of art should be preserved in an English public collection and some sacrifice of public money should be made to secure this end. But there is no reason to suppose that today the art-loving public in England will be inspired to throw away money on redeeming a Leonardo for the purpose of keeping the moribund Royal Academy in business. The authorities have done their best to conceal this, but in fact *the ransom money demanded* (my italics) will be used to no other purpose.' Of course such venom as this spurts out without effect.

We were in daily touch with our lawyers, the Charity Commissioners and the Treasury, taking the while the poisoned arrows on the broad shield of our sure and certain conviction. However I sometimes wonder that these attacks did not wear us down or deviate us from our clear course. But how should crude assailings, envy, bitterness and misrepresentation succeed when having all the facts to hand, one knows that with nothing hidden, one is right and, if I may say so, in the simple sense of the word, blameless.

There were a few heartening comments it is true, to mitigate the widespread abuse. Lord Cranbrook sent us a generous cheque. In the accompanying letter he said he would be grateful if we would place 2s. 6d. from our petty cash in the Leonardo cartoon collecting box. The remainder was to be a donation to our general funds, 'as a small token of his appreciation for the generosity of the Academicians in offering the cartoon to the nation at less than half its market value.' By this time we had heard that there was in Washington a syndicate of wealthy collectors who were prepared to bid up to £2,500,000 if the cartoon were auctioned — and yet the Academy was accused of greed!

How strange sometimes seem to be the values we place on things. For nearly two hundred years this great work had remained on our walls with only the normal careful protection. But when the magic words 'one million pounds' were sounded from the housetops, abnormal care had to be exercised. For greater safety it was removed to our vaults. Lord Crawford then asked us to lend it for display at the National Gallery from where the Appeal was to be conducted during the three months ahead. It left Burlington House early one morning before the traffic was about, under police escort, in the greatest secrecy and was set up, protected by a supposedly unbreakable sheet of perspex as well as being roped off at a distance of many feet. It was guarded by several attendants all the time and had electronic devices attached. While in the National Gallery it was visited by long queues of people anxious to see it. The attendance was hoisted by a quarter of a million — more than 40,000 reproductions of it were sold and just about every record in the fund-raising book were broken. A hundred times more people therefore saw it while it was there than when it was on constant exhibition in our Diploma Galleries for seventy years and until the second World War changed our plans for its display.

In spite of the commendable care taken by the authorities at Trafalgar Square, a lunatic hurled a bottle of ink at the cartoon breaking the perspex shield. The news of this filled me with alarm and I rushed up to the National Gallery with Humphrey Brooke in a state of great trepidation. We were taken up to the Conservation department and were mightily relieved to see only a minute fracture not more than a quarter inch square which could readily be repaired. Even stricter precautions were then taken and no fresh madman appeared.

Before the display Humphrey Brooke had given final approval, on our behalf, of all the measures taken under the direction of Sir Philip Hendy for the picture's safety. He had reported to me: 'It is perfectly safe — unless,' he added prophetically, 'a madman hurls a bottle of ink at it!'

Although money came in from all over the country it gradually became evident that the target was not going to be reached and that the government would be obliged to make up the difference. This finally proved to be the case.

When the time allocated for the National Appeal was at the eleventh hour, the Prime Minister urgently asked if I would go to see him. He wanted the Academy to extend the time-limit. I had to turn him down — the most I would do was to suggest an extra fortnight as I did not want the Leonardo's future to drag in the dust of doubt any longer. I explained that Lord Crawford had at the first declared, in a letter to us, that the time allocated was 'about right', that the Appeal had lost its initial impetus and that I had no mandate from the Academy Assembly for an extension of time. Mr Macmillan then complained that we were asking too much and said he had been told 'on indisputable evidence' the state of the Cartoon was not very good. I denied both these points and as regards the latter the Cartoon was afterwards examined by an international committee of conservators who declared it to be, considering its age, 'in a good condition'. Another lie nailed down, therefore.

Our meeting was held in the Cabinet Room at Admiralty

House, No 10 being then under reconstruction. It was attended only by the P.M. and me, together with his Secretary and the Secretary of the Royal Academy. As we talked, Mr Macmillan sipped sherry from a solitary glass — we were not invited to participate. He looked pale and tired. The room was in some disorder, the chairs awry and papers scattered on the table top. I felt he was not entirely with us. There was something ominous in the dark silhouette of his profile as it appeared to me against the windows overlooking Horse Guards Parade on that fine summer morning. The encounter was brief, sharp and uncompromising. But the Prime Minister was very courteous. He personally took us to the door. The oblique lines of his hooded eyes seemed more oblique than ever and made them look unusually sad. His wonted smile seemed a little strained.

A few hours after we had left Whitehall we were buying newspapers carrying sensational news of great Cabinet changes. The Lord Chancellor, the Chancellor of the Exchequer and other leading Ministers had been dismissed. The Prime Minister had had more on his plate that morning than a work of art — a masterpiece for which America would have delved into a bottomless pocket, and which had smiled on our House for 200 years almost and which was to save our threatened independence.

There was an air of drama and unreality in the atmosphere of that day. Brooke and I were asked to wait a few minutes in a small vaulted room in the Admiralty in which, I was told, the body of Nelson lay the night before his burial in St Paul's Cathedral. Then there was this strange encounter. Again, in the evening, a newspaper telephoned to ask me if, when I had gone to see the P.M. that morning he had offered me a Ministry of Fine Arts. 'Good God, no,' I replied. 'When bureaucracy enters the Temple of the Arts at one door, I shall go out at another.'

When on the day appointed, Lord Crawford came to Burlington House and handed me the first cheque for £400,000 I could not look at it. Humphrey understood and kindly took it away. I felt like a Judas Iscariot and my heart was sick. David Crawford who had personally conducted the whole Appeal and had collected more money for such a cause than had ever been achieved before, his battle over, one of the most beautiful pictures in the world saved for Great Britain, went straight from Burlington House to hospital. The surgeons wanted him. He had kept them waiting until the task he had so nobly undertaken had been completed.

I went back to my studio and, I must confess, wept like a child.

CHAPTER EIGHT

TWO
LIEUTENANTS

TOWARD THE END of the 1920s I was engaged in so many sculptural projects that my Chelsea studio, plus one I had in Kensington, became insufficient. And so I bought a house in Tregunter Road which had a long garden stretching down to Cathcart Road. This made possible the building of a studio at the bottom of the garden with its own entrance from the other road. We lived in the house for ten years while our children grew up. I added on a studio for Muriel. She then had more time for painting and sculpting than before or since. In those days we could get good domestic help. We were able to entertain our many friends and I think the ten years spent there before the war were the happiest of my life.

Lilies, roses and sulphur coloured evening primroses grew lavishly in the garden and a fine old mulberry tree fruited lusciously every year without fail. Carol and I, dressed in bathing costumes, used to climb its branches to collect the squashy, purple-juiced, delicious berries of a summer evening and then get into a bath to remove the stains. The application of lemon juice bleached with ease the more stubborn patches. Mulberries and cream for breakfast taken on the dining room balcony while the morning sun poured down on us was frequently our reward.

Halcyon days were those. I was, at the time, carving great blocks of Portland Stone on the Bank of England and India House and making bronzes for South Africa House and Threadneedle Street. The sound of children laughing in the garden, the sound of the hammering of stone in the studio, my wife and I visiting each other's studios every day — sometimes sitting for each other — and spending long evenings together, the propinquity of friends, concerts, theatres and galleries within easy reach, ideas flowing freely and with opportunity to carry them out, all contributed to the cheerful sense of the rightness of things. And then the war came.

Soon after the war ended we sold the house in which we had been so happy in a better world. By building a wall across the garden I retained my studio and was able to add to it a small flat. To build this flat necessitated cutting down the mulberry tree — alas! This is on my conscience as one of the black deeds of my life. Then we sought a house in the country. The house, we stipulated to the agent, must be within an hour's reach of Chelsea, had to be small, standing in its own grounds with sufficient grazing to keep my daughter's horse. We found Weavers in Surrey, two miles from the nearest village, and have lived there ever since. The house, which has been developed from two Tudor cottages, is in the parish of Blechingley, but two miles distant from its medieval church. This contains an exceptionally fine baroque tomb (1705) of Sir Robert Clayton, a Lord Mayor of London. Two miles away in the other direction and on the top of the Downs is the very small Gothic church of St Peter and St Paul at Chaldon, which has an early thirteenth-century *Doom* covering the west wall. The sophistication of the Clayton tomb and the primitive *Doom* mural painting seem to me to symbolise the contrast between the two subjects of this Chapter.

We have found this country retreat an invaluable asset during the years of my Presidency and intensive sculptural activity for it is remote (though less than 20 miles from Westminster Bridge) and quiet. Being fond of walking I have spent many hours roaming the hills, walking along the Pilgrim's Way, across ploughed fields and in the little woods. And I have painted the landscapes and skyscapes. In doing these things I have found refreshment for body and spirit. Muriel loves the quietness there and Carol the riding of and caring for horses. Carol, Muriel and I each have a small studio at Weavers. Carol took a course in painting at the Academy Schools and has painted a number of excellent horse pictures.

But to return to the studio in London which has been the centre of my work for nearly forty years. When in 1930 it was being planned, I was given a commission to make bronze doors for the Bank of England. They had to be 20 feet high and so its proportions had perforce to be changed to accommodate the large models. Many tons of clay, of stone and bronze have been used within its walls since it was built.

Every artist feels that after a time his studio takes on a personality of its own and when one has become so familiar with it as, after so many years, I have with mine, its bricks and mortar do not make it into everything it is. People feel this with houses — of course, when they become their homes. My studio's oak floor, brick walls and pent roof with its large skylights are but the limbs and features of a creature which has a warm and friendly heart. It is staunch, strong, masculine and honest standing by me faithfully and serving every demand made upon it. I have felt it ready at all times to greet me with open arms. If it died in a fire tomorrow it could not be resurrected from the plans which still exist. Something which had lived would have gone for ever, something which has emanated from a hundred thousand hours of labour, from ideas which have taken formal shape in it and pale unborn schemes half-thought but never crystalised, from successes and failures, hopes and fears, friends, events, small and large, and a myriad of tiny things which the great arm of Time has brought together to create an aura and saturate the studio fabric with an essence indescribable but real.

With the new studio teeming with work, my assistants asked for some unskilled hand who would do odd jobs and keep the place clean. An ex-soldier was found. He had seen seven years of service in India, was upstanding, good-looking and muscular. He would do, I thought, for a month's trial. How that month and how that trial developed you, my readers, shall hear if you care to read on. William Stafford Chadwick was his name. It soon became 'Chaddy' to us all. Chaddy swept floors, attended to stoves, beat up the modelling clay, went on errands, brewed excellent tea and was general factotum. He was often called on to help in the house as well as studio.

From the first our children loved him, for he was kind and gentle as well as strong. He often carried Carol, four or five years old then, on his back while she pretended he was a horse. For her, my son, my wife and me he would do anything for the rest of his life. Whether it were to buy goldfish, search London for a particular coloured budgerigar, make tiny stables or shop straw for the rabbit hutch he would do these things with an endearing willingness. He would dig in the garden which separated the house from the studio, take Carol to Battersea Dog's Home to see the stray creatures they both cared for or fetch potatoes for the kitchen if the cook had run short, and he did them, and a hundred other things with that grace which comes from a genuine sense of service. Later on he would hold Carol's horse, fence her paddock — for then we were living in the country — help to build a fountain and cut down trees. His service was willing but never servile, his gait slow and deliberate, and he had a manner and smile, which attracted him to everyone from tradesmen to princes and from the borough dustmen to the Queen's secretary, so that when he died, from all quarters came tributes to his character. Chadwick was devoted to me as I was to him. We became friends and his zeal for the studio and all its ways was unfailing. He told me once, when in hospital, his greatest desire was to feel the studio floor beneath his feet again. If ever there was a genuine, if ever an honest man it was Chaddy, if ever — in the simple sense — a good man it was Chaddy. His constant good humour pleased us and his many malapropisms delighted and amused us, as did his fund of anecdotes.

He was very proud of his father, who was a taxi-driver, and often referred to the parental words of wisdom. His father's father,

43. R.A.F. Memorial, Valetta, Malta.

44. Detail of Plate 43.

45. Four of the *Seve*

nt Navy memorial, Tower Hill.

46. Artist's wife: red sandstone.

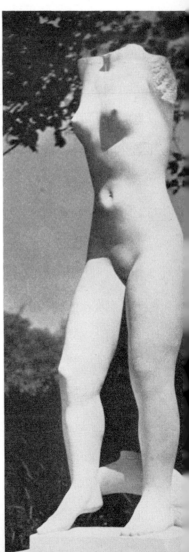

47. *Aphrodite II:* at the Tate Gallery, on exhibition at Battersea Park.

tramping the country in search of work, died on the roadside from starvation and his mother, a woman of great age and considerable size, survived him when he died at 61 after being in my employ for 35 years. He would sometimes remind me that he was only 'on a month's trial'. He produced a family of four children from a wife who was 'nanny' to my daughter and it was when they were both employed by us that they got married.

Chadwick was taken on when he was 26. He was unskilled but gradually picked up the technical requirements of a sculptor's studio. Being strong he relieved me of much weight-lifting. He learned how to make armatures — the supporting structure for clay models — to do rough carpentry and became very proficient in plaster-casting. He took over responsibilities with the bronze-founders and stone and marble merchants and developed as I have already indicated 'a way with him' in his management of the many and various contacts incumbent upon a studio life. In dealing with the office of the Royal Academy, with the Bank Manager — whoever you will — he was equally efficient, good humoured and at ease. At times he would be called to the telephone while wearing an overall covered in plaster and would whisper to me *en passant*: 'Shall I put on my striped trousers first?'

A little while before Chadwick died he measured the hollow in the wood block floor below the door separating the two main studios and told me with a sort of pride-cum-satisfaction that between us we had worn away $\frac{3}{16}$ of an inch of oak in our comings and goings. He thought the oak blocks more than an inch thick would last us out! Oftentimes he worked while in much pain, but complained very little. When it became really bad I tried to persuade him to go into hospital, but this he would not do. True to form he refused to give in till all the heavy plaster casting — taking many months — for the New Zealand sculptures was finished at the end of 1965. Only then would he pay his doctor the visit which I believe he knew presaged his end. It did and so died a noble soul.

From the grandson of an ill-starred peasant I turn now to a son of an ancient line of prosperous Yorkshire wool merchants. From a cockney lad to a graduate of Magdalene. It is with gratitude that I record my great indebtedness to another real friend, Humphrey Brooke. Without the good fortune of having him as a colleague it would have been impossible for me to fulfil the double role of sculptor and P.R.A. We have travelled a ten-year long and rough road together, planned many a campaign, fought, sometimes won and often lost battles. All the while we have remained joint advocates for the same cause — the promotion of the Fine Arts and the honour and glory of the Royal Academy.

Presidents come and go but the Brookes of our Institution go on if not for ever, at least for a very long time. There have been only seven secretaries in 200 years of our existence. When I was a trustee of the Tate Gallery, 1942–49, H.B. was Assistant Director. Certain things were happening there at that time, of which I and my fellow trustee and fellow member of the Academy, Henry Lamb the painter, very much disapproved. Humphrey did not stand, to us, on the dark side of the picture. When a few years afterwards he offered himself as candidate for the secretaryship of the Royal Academy, Henry Lamb and I, both being members of the Council at the time, were able to tell of his admirable record at Millbank. But apart from our recommendation Brooke stood out head and shoulders from the other applicants and was the obvious choice. Therefore he took Walter Lamb's chair and has since filled it with ample physical, efficient mental and characterful completeness. I'm glad he quarrelled with John Rothenstein and came to us.

The waters about Burlington House were comparatively calm during Lamb's regime. While Brooke and I have worked in it together the enervating, still waters of complacency have been succeeded by dangerous, turbulent waves, whipped up by the winds of change that have everywhere blown about the world. If the passage has been rough it has nevertheless been exciting. Happily we have seen eye to eye in all the major decisions which have had to be made during our working years together. If this had not been so we should not have come through the heavy weather. Small differences due to frayed nerves have always ended in mutual respect. I am sure that I could not have endured the strain of office had it not been that Humphrey was there to support me. If my successor has my good fortune in this particular, then that will be well for all of us.

His single-minded devotion to the Royal Academy is the chief secret of his success. He tells me the schoolboy visits he made to our exhibitions in his teens inspired him and no doubt are at the root of his tireless and enthusiastic labours in the mounting of many of the great Winter Exhibitions of the past 15 years. For the annual Summer Exhibitions he works with equal zest. This devotion is infectious and is shared by all members of the staff at Burlington House. Our institution, being an unbureaucratic body, infuses a sense of personal involvement into us all. It is remarkable how the staff, from the porters upwards, respond to any call we make on their time and energies. One feels they are motivated by a true concern for our affairs and that our interests are their interests too. There does not exist that master–man tension which bedevils so many of the problems of employment.

Only recently the Academy Council decided to open the galleries on Sunday mornings to accommodate the huge crowds who came to see the Pierre Bonnard exhibition. Members of the staff were unanimous in their acquiescence. The new arrangement meant, of course, longer hours, but they did not mind any more than Humphrey minds working at all times of the day and night if need be for the welfare of the Academy; not even minding taking umbrellas on a wet Sunday when queues stretching from away down Piccadilly and across the courtyard sought admission to the Goya Exhibition. Humphrey can handle a dripping umbrella as adroitly as he can a Fleet Street Editor or a recalcitrant member. May the day be far away when he relinquishes his job.

CHAPTER NINE

SITTERS

PORTRAIT SCULPTURE is a branch of the Art which has a fascination of its own and I have made many sculptural likenesses. There are many excellent sculptors making busts in England today and it was to encourage them that I helped to found the Society of Portrait Sculptors in 1953 and became its first President.

My youngest 'sitter' was my daughter whom I modelled when she was only three days old. The perfect skull formation, crumpled ears and only half opened eyes made an intriguing study. The next youngest was my son Robin whose bust I made when he was nine months. It was made at a lean time, in fact I was working on the clay on that memorable morning when Rudyard Kipling called. He showed intelligent interest in it, examining it from many angles. His father was, as is well known, an art master in India and as his mother was a sister of Lady Burne-Jones, the Fine Arts were not strange to him. He told me that at the request of Burne-Jones and with the aid of an English woman doctor his father was able to make a collection of plaster casts of the feet of Indian temple girls, feet which had never been cramped and mis-shapen by the wearing of shoes. The collection had disappeared he said and added: 'I commission you to find them before you die'. Perfection of the hands and feet was a Burne-Jones fetish. I have failed in all my enquiries about the collection.

The plaster cast of the bust of Robin was sent to the Academy but rejected, it was sent again with the same result. It had a sadness in the expression which suggested to me 'The Infant Christ', so putting a halo on the head I called it that, cast it in bronze and submitted it again. This time it was accepted and bought by the Chantry Bequest. An artist's wife is, of course, fair game and mine sat for me many times, sweetly, patiently and tirelessly. She has never failed in any demand I have made on her.

In 1960 the Council of the Academy commissioned me to make a marble bust of the Queen for its collection of Royal portraits. Her Majesty gave me six sittings of an hour each at my studio. She came without fuss, alone except for a detective, and Muriel was there to help with her cloak. No sitter could have been more considerate to any artist. During the sittings she spoke of many things in a way which almost made me forget that she wore a crown.

Yehudi Menuhin was a delightful sitter also. In a letter to me he wrote: 'I can think of nothing more pleasant than sitting quietly, removed in your studio from all worldly disturbances, while you handle that wonderful basic material which is clay.' The gentle calmness of his manner, the thoughtful quietness of his conversation, while he sat with feet tucked up like a Buddha, made the sittings very memorable. I remember him carrying his Stradivarius once and placing it in its case very close to his chair. He asked me to make a bronze of his wife, but dear Diana refused to sit because she said she was too thin (which was nonsense) and that her mother used to tell her she was only 'two profiles stuck together'. I expect the phrase was really her own; she is full of like amusing remarks such as 'Yehudi is abroad scraping for a living' and—writing in a transcontinental American train at a time when Yehudi refused to fly — 'I'm tired of riding on square wheels'. Yehudi's enjoyment of the peacefulness of an artist's studio calls to mind a story that Malcolm Sargent told me of when he was sitting to A. K. Lawrence for his portrait. He said he envied A.K. being removed from the hurly-burly of rehearsals for concerts, to which A.K. replied: 'How can you say that, I'd give ten years of my life if people would gather round my pictures and clap.'

Montague Norman came for his bust, which the Bank of England commissioned when he retired after his 20 years as Governor. His had a fine head with an unusually handsome profile in which the obtuse angle between forehead and nose gave special character. He would be driven to sittings by Priscilla, his wife, who usually stayed while he sat and at times would soothe his aching temples with her gently stroking fingers for a serious operation had left an aftermath of pain. I asked this almost legendary man of great power and influence, this Prince of Bankers, when he would give me another sitting. He pointed to Priscilla and said: 'Ask her, she wears the trousers'; and so it is with most of us. He lived then at Thorpe Lodge, a house he built for himself on Campden Hill. His drawing room had a barrel-shaped ceiling. He had asked his architect to make it so because when in South Africa as a young man, being ill with a fever he was conveyed across the veldt in a trek wagon and there and then determined that if he got better he would build a house with a ceiling to remind him of the cover of the wagon at which he had to gaze through many rough miles having a raging temperature the while. He also built a large music room in which we were invited to hear vocal and chamber works. The most memorable for Muriel and me was lieder singing by Kathleen Ferrier with Gerald Moore accompanying.

Augustus John made an unconventional painting of Norman for the Bank which they didn't like. It is a fine thing and will one day be brought up from the cellars to which it was confined and recognised for the work of art it is. Norman complained to me that John would quite casually cry off a sitting even when, at great inconvenience, one of the leading bankers of the world would arrive by appointment on the artist's doorstep. While painting Montague Norman in the mornings he was painting Tallulah Bankhead in the afternoons and his interest in the two sitters was apparently unequally divided.

One of the most modest men who came for his bust was Lord Hives. His likeness had been commissioned by Messrs Rolls-Royce for their head office in Derby. He had risen from the shop floor to the Chairmanship of the world-renowned company. I was told his office door was always left ajar and without any difficulty or any previous arrangement any of the staff, from the lowest to the highest, could walk in and find him ready for the airing of any grievance or the discussion of any problems which had arisen. More than most of my sitters, he must have thought a sculptor's studio to be an odd place!

I was commissioned during the second World War to make bronzes of several prominent sailors. I thought I should discover the naval type of physiognomy, but was soon disillusioned for they were all widely different. They were of course all deeply involved in the war and I could get them for only half-an-hour during their lunch time. Therefore I had an improvised studio set up in Admiralty Arch over its middle and the captains and Admirals would come to sit. The most difficult to get was Admiral of the Fleet Lord Mountbatten; in fact I never secured him. Several times appointments were made only to be cancelled almost at the last minute. I think he was working 22 hours out of every 24 in those tragic days.

The next was Admiral Vian. He said firmly he wouldn't sit, though he was officially told he must. After much protesting he agreed to give me a grudging half hour, 'but I must get on with my papers', he declared. The sitting started gloomily for he had his head bent down reading and I in a state of nerves tried this way and that to get a look at him. At last the clay began to fly and I made pretence of doing something. A sidelong glance at what the sculptor fellow was at and then on with his documents again. As the clay model began to shape the glancing increased and the reading decreased till he finally put his papers under the seat of his trousers and spent the rest of the sitting looking on and talking affably enough. Finally, looking at his watch, said he must be off and dashed out of the studio into the main building. When he had disappeared I noticed he had left his papers behind on the chair and to my alarm they were marked 'Top Secret'. Although I feared they might burn my fingers I picked them up and rushed after him only to find as I entered a long corridor at one end, that Vian was at the other agitatedly running towards me.

I feel lucky to be alive after meeting that dashing sailor. Before the first sitting I went to see him at his house at Liphook. After luncheon he drove me back to the railway station at such a speed through narrow twisting roads that I feared for my life; the while his two young daughters egged him on with cries of delight and 'Go on, Daddy, faster'.

When I made the Jellicoe Memorial Fountain for Trafalgar Square I also made a bust of him which is placed against the north wall alongside one of Admiral Beatty. Lutyens, the architect, told me that Lady Jellicoe was irate at the proposal to place her husband in the same square as an Admiral of whom, it is a euphemism to say, she did not approve. But Lut said I must show her the bust and be prepared for a violently prejudiced visitor when she came. However, when she did come, I arranged for my wife to greet her in the house and bring her down to the studio. Muriel entered into the arrangement and took her first into her own studio, showed her paintings she had made of our children and channelled the conversation to children in general and in particular to Lady Jellicoe's own grand-children, of whom we knew she was extremely fond. This talk of children did the trick for she arrived in my studio in a very good mood indeed. Catching a glimpse of the clay model in the room beyond she exclaimed, 'How wonderful — it's exactly like him,' and sending for her chauffeur asked him if he did not think so too. She then sent him back for Admiral Bacon's *Life of Jellicoe* in which she wrote appreciatively and presented it to me. Next time I saw Lutyens he declared that my name should be Wheedler, not Wheeler.

Herbert Baker asked me to make a bronze bust of T. E. Lawrence (Lawrence of Arabia), who at the time called himself Shaw and was an aircraftsman in the R.A.F. Of himself, when we first met, he said: 'No name — just a number'. There was only one sitting, but that was of five hours' duration. It was on a cold November day in 1929. He would not sit but stood the whole time — like a rock. His eyes were small and seemed to be shrunken back into his head. The result of the eastern sun or the midnight oil lamp perhaps. His chin was large, but not so prominent as John portrayed it and there was a marked ridge of the frontal bone of his forehead running parallel to his eyebrows, so marked that I told him I thought I would put in a cyclops eye below it. 'Oh, don't do that', he said in a tone that made me think he would like me to have done so. Seeing that I was modelling his neck he took off his tunic so that I could see it more easily. Then to help me with the modelling of his shoulders he divested himself of his shirt and stood naked to the waist. Noticing a contorted collar bone I asked him if it had been broken to which he replied: 'I've had most of my bones broken.' Then I noticed what few can have seen, large white weals round the thorax made by the lashes of the whips before he was thrown by the Turks in a blood tub for dead.

At one point he was called to the telephone, and on returning he reported: 'That was Nancy Astor. She wants me to go to lunch. I've had orders to drop her — and in any case your wife is giving me lunch, isn't she?' Again: 'I'm translating Homer, a lot of it is mere jingle.'

The small room in which he wrote and slept above Baker's office was littered with books. He was constantly sent new books for comment or review. He told me that one day he found it practically impossible to get into bed, so he filled his knapsack with the most recent novels and made nocturnal visits to Canons' houses in Westminster Abbey Close to deposit those volumes which he thought most suitable in the most appropriate letter-boxes. His presence at No 14, Barton Street was kept a secret from the general public. But one morning the telephone bell rang and a voice announced: 'Is Colonel Lawrence there — I am George Bernard Shaw.' The duteous office boy slapped down the receiver with 'Tell that to the Marines'. Ten minutes later a loud knocking at the door heralded G.B.S. in person.

The enigma of this strange, romantic figure arose I thought from a dual personality in him. One side loved literature, art and the hermit's cell while the other craved action and the limelight. They were at odds with each other, the former despising the latter for its vulgar inclination. There was no doubt about his peculiar fascination which affected all with whom he came into contact. On whatever subject he spoke, and they were many and various, he did so with seeming authority. The last time I saw him was when he climbed with me up the ladders at the Bank of England, where I had been working for months, to see, behind tarpaulins, the large stone statues I had carved on the Threadneedle Street façade. They had been severely criticised by one of the directors and the opinion of Lawrence of Arabia was thought to be sufficiently authoritative (even on matters of art) to quell opposition or uphold it. Rather like, 100 years earlier, the Iron Duke's opinions were indisputable. Fortunately for me his verdict was favourable, the director was properly put in his place and my sculptures remained in theirs.

It was a pleasure to sculpt Sir Donald Wolfit for he has a fine head to work on. Sittings were made more enjoyable for me when he would speak lines from the great Shakespearian plays while I modelled. At any time his sonorous voice is good to hear and the studio walls and the sculptor responded sympathetically. If a wife has to view a portrait on completion the artist is usually in nervous tension. So it was when Lady Wolfit came. If she is pleased he is relieved so that when the charming Rosalind approved, I was naturally delighted. But whether it be a wife, relatives or a committee which comes to see a portrait, the artist always breathes a sigh of relief when that hurdle has been taken. Opinions on likeness differ so. One will think the nose too small, another, too large. One will say: 'It's just like so and so seen from here', another that 'from over there I can see him when he is such and such a mood'. John Singer Sargent is (among others) credited with the remark: 'A portrait is a picture in which there is something wrong with the mouth.'

One of the best things that can happen, so I have found, is for a large committee to view the portraiture together. I remember such a meeting when I had made a bas-relief of Prebendary Wilson Carlile, founder of the Church Army, for St Paul's Cathedral.

Members of the Church Army began to file in at the door till I thought they would never cease. However, when nearly twenty critics stood around their comments cancelled each other out and so, for me at least, all went well. Even better than this was when I was making a bronze bust of William Paterson, the founder of the Bank of England. Only one tiny profile of him in the British Museum was all the likeness that could be obtained. When a committee came to see it there was a stony silence broken at last by its Chairman who said: 'To those of us who remember him its not bad, and anyhow he looks an excellent founder.'

Another victim whose voice made delicious hearing was Tom Bodkin, whose brazen likeness is now in the Barber Institute of the Birmingham University where as first Director he built up a remarkable collection of old masters. His constantly smiling mouth and bright blue eyes, his white beard and clear pink complexion together made a benign whole. He told me while sitting one day that in Birmingham the boys often called after him 'Father Christmas'. Strange to relate while we were waiting for a taxi on our way to the Athenaeum for lunch, when the sitting had ended, two little cockney boys in passing looked up at him and said: 'Hello, Faver Christmas.' 'I told you so,' said Tom to me and chuckled with glee. Tom was not only a great character but a leading art critic and art historian. I always considered him to be one of those sensible and sound critics whose numbers could be counted on the finger's of one's hands. When one has strong likes and dislikes one is bound to be wrong sometimes, and though that was the case with Bodkin, he was most often right.

The first portrait bust I was commissioned to make was while I was still a student at the R.C.A. and it proved to be one of the happiest though with a sad sequel. John Perry, the then Professor of Civil Engineering at the adjacent Royal College of Science, asked me to make a bronze of his nephew of eight or nine years old. I had already made Perry's portrait (on the 'Perry Medal'). He had a beautiful head loaded with curls — a veritable young Eros — and we had riotous and amusing sittings together. In an endeavour to keep his restlessness in check I would occasionally throw a pellet of clay on to the wall and so arrest his gaze for a moment. But when *he* wanted clay pellets to throw, the sitting came to an abrupt end. As I built up, pellet by pellet, his head formation, he said: 'Are you putting in my brains?' I agreed. 'How many are you giving me?' 'About a hundred,' I replied. 'Will that do?' 'Oh, yes,' said the happy child. 'Nurse sometimes says I haven't any.' After a short silence, 'Do you know what I'm going to do with my statue [sic] when I grow up — I'm going to knock a hole in the mouth and use it as a money-box.' Uncle Perry had the bronze and I kept a replica which many years after I showed at Burlington House. It was bought by the boy's mother, who did not know of the copy, but was overjoyed to have it because that lovely boy had died while at Eton.

There are still some people who think busts are made only of deceased persons. This story is told of the late Alfred Drury. He was travelling by train when a fellow passenger asked him if he knew an artist who would paint the Mayor of his town. When Drury suggested that instead a sculptor might be commissioned to make a bust, the objection came: 'But our Mayor is still living!'

CHAPTER TEN

GUIDES, COUNSELLORS AND FRIENDS

TO THOSE WHO have been given a large cornucopia of friends, life is rich and good, and I am one of them. I am ever mindful of the warmth they have given to my life. If it were possible I would pay tribute to all and each, but that being impracticable between the covers of one small book, I must be content with a truncated catalogue and confine myself with references to a few more particularly concerned with my upbringing, my development as an artist and to those of my mature years. Mere adumbration of their portraiture may not be acceptable, and will certainly be inadequate, but what it will lack in truth to nature will be due to an unpractised hand and against my best intent.

I must put aside the temptation to dwell upon those close friends who have brought warmth and sweetness into our family life. That dear Yorkshire lad and lass, Dorothy and George Quarmby. Fellow Wulfrunian, water-colour painter, Sidney Causer, who with his family occupied a house adjacent to ours on the clifftop at Fairlight, where during the second World War, we were forced to live because our London house had been bombed. Many merry evenings we spent with these — with Harry Parr and Kate Parr and with Malcolm Osborne, R.A. and Amy his wife. Numerous others, too.

Firstly then that early influence and copy-book schoolmaster —
head of my elementary Church School of St Lukes, Blakenhall,
Wolverhampton. 'Daddy Barcroft', we called him, an affectionate
appellation of one who was benevolence itself. Besides initiating
me into the three 'R's', he gave me my first lessons in drawing.
For these I attended evening classes held once a week in the dining
room of his modest villa in Villiers Street. My father paid him a
small fee and so did a dozen or so other papas for their hopeful
offsprings and I've no doubt the fractional addition to what in
those days must have been a miserable salary was a very welcome
reward for the sacrifice of his evening's quiet after the day's effort
to instil knowledge into not very receptive noddles.

In those far off days when soldiers wore scarlet coats and women
seemed to be solid to the ground, headmasters donned tall silk
hats and square-cut frock coats when they went to the schoolhouse.
He was no exception. Shutting my eyes I can see him now so
garbed. He is portly and has a rubicund face, very dignified and
stern-seeming and he carries a large, silver-mounted walking stick
as he leaves his house and with dignified steps moves down hill to
the school. His whole bearing is becoming to so 'great' a man. We
respected, but not feared, him. His voice was rich, deep and kindly
and for me his influence was wholly beneficial. If I was ever
reproved I'm sure it was gently done and, although he had not had
all the advantages of modern educational developments, I believe
he was an ideal schoolmaster for the 'young idea' at that time and
in that place.

His evening classes provided high lights to my boyhood days
not 'with satchel and shining morning face creeping like snail
unwill ngly to school', but with bubbling excitement, having
swallowed a high tea, I would, clutching my drawing book, run
all the way — a mile perhaps — to drawing class in Villiers Street.
Dear old Daddy Barcroft, what fresh-lit fires you fanned in me
and how you boasted when your pupil of 12 was admitted to the
Art School at younger years than the regulations would have it.
It was you, too, who taught me to write 'copper-plate' on

imitation cheque forms. You said: 'Now make out a cheque for £100' and I thought this fabulous wealth. You said: 'Your copper plate is excellently done', but you would give a heavy sigh if now you saw my present almost illegible cursive hand. Though your name is not written upon the scroll of learning I am gratefully recording it here.

If 'Daddy Barcroft' developed my childish drawing, 'Poppa Sheldon', to whom I have already referred, shone a golden light upon the pages of English Literature which had first been opened for me when my father read to us on the family hearth and encouraged us to take down from his shelves and read whichever books we wished and whenever we liked to do so. I sometimes dream that had I not, with blinkers on, so urgently followed in the paths of the Mistress Art, I could have been a servitor in the Temple of the Muses because, though I took scarcely a step upon the road that leads to Helicon, I found the prospect glorious and fascinating. Sheldon, too, was gently spoken. He had no technique of control so that my class mates at the Higher Grade School, to which I was sent from St Luke's, were habitually unruly. Many a time did I think I saw him wince under the lash of their disdain for the knowledge he would have us absorb and I hated them for it. I think I did better in other subjects, but the one I really loved was Poppa Sheldon's 'English'. I wish I had, in later years, found him out to thank him for those schoolday peeps into the jewel casket of poetry. But now he is dead, and another sin of omission has been added to my account.

My love of poetry was fostered a few years later by a fellow student at the Art School. I well remember him turning to me on one of our walks and saying: 'If you don't read poetry, you miss half the joy in life.' With that he took me to Barker's bookshop in Queens Square and presented me with copies of Tennyson and Palgrave's *Golden Treasury*. I turn over their dog-eared pages now, remembering him with thankfulness while receiving from them ever fresh delight. He and I would spend happy hours in Barker's where the friendly manager had a care for us young students and from where volumes in the Everyman's Library could be bought for one shilling apiece. My friend's name, I fear, will mean nothing to anybody now but I would like to write it down — Horace L. Rubery. He painted tolerable watercolours, left the art school after amorous excursions and went to live in Italy where he married a beautiful signorita and later disappeared from my ken. Rubery and I would sometimes take midnight walks by moonlight into Baggeridge Woods for we were both romantics, together roaming the fields of sentiment unashamed and collecting anthologies of sweet rhymes, beneath great trees long since cut down to secure the coal beneath — the dead bones of their progenitors of the Carboniferous Age.

Of Robert Jackson Emerson. There were many occasions on which, in his presence, I was able to pay tribute to this remarkable teacher who leaving the cobblers last to which he had been apprenticed, took up handfuls of clay and of pupils and moulded them all into shapeliness. He became a sculptor of distinction and teacher of rare ability for he had the gift of instruction and was able to impart to his pupils something of his own passion for the art of Phydias and Michelangelo. When he came to the Wolverhampton School of Art as Second Master, he swept through the place like a flame. The school had been going along pleasantly, even drowsily enough. We were comfortable and complacent. He changed it in a trice. No longer was it to be tepid, but boiling with enthusiasm. From having a general desire to become an artist I turned under Emerson into a devotee of sculpture; his appointment as master was therefore one of the main turning points in my life.

He was a very small man with a large head and humped shoulders. His deep set eyes shone like lamps beneath the over-hanging brows of a high forehead. His meal times were very short and the hours spent in his studio and the school were very long. When his many successful students returned to Wolverhampton, they knew that 'Bob' would be there waiting with a rich gift of good fellowship and that they could talk to him about things

48. Dr Thomas Bodkin;
Barber Institute, Birmingham
University.

49. *The Offspring:* carving from
branching pearwood.

50. The Elements, *Earth* and *Water*: Government offices, Whitehall.

51. The erecting of part of Plate 50 watched by the author and his assistant, Chadwick.

52. Bronze statue symbolising power: English Electric House, The Strand.

53. Equestrian study: piaffe.

55. Barclay's Bank, Lombard Street.

54. Yehudi Menuhin: bronze bust

56. Armature showing the preliminary construction of the large *Hercules and the Lion* for Barclays Bank, Lombard Street.

which seemed to us all to be the only ones that mattered — the Arts, a subject about which few others in our prosperous town cared one jot. A notable exception was the proprietor of the *Express and Star*, Norrie Graham, who gave Emerson a studio in his newspaper premises. We often met there, Norrie, Bob, Muriel and I with a few others of like mind — Peter Silvers and Sidney Causer among them; while the Wulfrunian business of living, of making motor cars and money went on around us, we built an ivory tower in Castle Street. In it, however, we worked like Trojans above the printing presses on the floor below.

Emerson's teaching of sculpture became almost a legend in the art schools of the country because of the numerous successes of his pupils, several of whom won the Prix de Rome and many more places at the Royal College of Art. Several of them are now masters of sculpture in the 'Art Colleges' which have replaced the 'Schools' in this 'improved' land of ours.

Douglas St Leger is an architect now living in Cape Town. I met him as I was finishing my studentship and he, working then as an assistant to Herbert Baker, encouraged Baker to commission me to make various of my early sculptures. I am indebted to him particularly because he persuaded me to carve direct in stone. On the Winchester Memorial Cloisters Baker asked me to sculpt the Madonna and Child for a niche facing The Meads. It was to be life size and cut in Portland stone. I proposed to proceed the safe way by a method known as 'pointing'. St Leger urged the bolder *modus operandi*. I hesitated because as a beginner I thought I might have ruined the block and then I should have to bear the expense, which I couldn't afford, of replacing it. Douglas at once offered to pay for another monolith if anything went wrong, through my inexperience, with the first. Such generosity led me to adopt the method which has many times since served my ends well.

Both Muriel and I wish we had not lost him and his charming wife Thea to South Africa where he has, among other things, designed important additions to St George's cathedral at Cape Town. Thea Chance is his second wife, his first marriage having failed. She was brought to us for vetting before their engagement. So different from her 'polite' Kensington predecessor she sat on our dining-room table swinging her legs and munching an apple which she consumed skin and core and all. Meanwhile, she held a resounding altercation with Douglas and concluded with: 'You're all right, Leger, but you're such a bloody hypocrite'. This pleased him more than all the soft endearing phrases of the properly brought up wife. They have lived happily ever after and still live perched up high and remote on Table Mountain overlooking the ocean. Two rare birds in their aerie.

At the core of the Academy's foundation are the Schools which we have maintained entirely ourselves and given free instruction for 200 years. Our scholars have included Turner, Constable, Blake, Flaxman and hundreds of well-known painters, sculptors and architects. The head of the Schools is called the Keeper, and there have been many famous Keepers including Fuseli, Charles Sims and so on. It was my good fortune when I was elected President to have Henry Rushbury as Keeper. He is a man of expert hand, the eye of an eagle and a wise and penetrating mind. Not only was he a fine headmaster of the Schools but his sound advice was always an invaluable guide to the Council, me and the other officers. During his Keepership the R.A. Schools prospered and added lustre to its reputation among the leading Art Colleges and Schools of the country.

I always sought Henry's views when those many opposing opinions and clashes of wills which are inevitable in an institution such as ours, rocked the boat. Composed of seventy to 80 egotists, as artists are, 'The Academy' has many views which have to be reconciled in the conduct of our affairs. After 12 years of great activity in our Schools and our Councils, Henry went to live at Lewes from where he wrote me the following letter.

Dec. 1964.

'My dear Charles,

'It was very kind of you to telephone Florence and to tell us the news of yesterday's meeting at the R.A. for you can imagine how anxious we were to know how it went.

'Long experience with R.A. meetings has taught me that you can never be sure. I am now content and feel we can jog along in fair comfort, and I look back on the R.A. and feel they have been generous to me as ever.

'Charles, you have always been friendly to me and made the last eight years of the Keepership pleasant and easy. You have gone out of your way to be appreciative of the way the Schools progressed even though you hated much of the work the students produced, as, of course, I did too. You can no longer dictate to students, they are fed on a strange fare of intellec- tualized cods wallop even before they enter the schools, and when in London the West End galleries swallow them up and they think they have arrived, as important artists, poor saps. Among them there are those who are serious and well worth while. Others fade into oblivion.

'I am wondering how the General Assembly developed. I understood that there was to be a mild revolt. The rebel group usually fizzles out for they are always looking over their shoulders, not trusting each other.

'In this world of tumult, change, and slick Alecs the R.A. will have a job to keep its head above water and there's always the danger of the 'take-over' bids from the enemies who have laid in wait for the climate to be in their favour. My dear Charles, the R.A. will last us out, and many more who come after. I wonder how the Mellon Collection struck you. I had only a brief look at it and thought it a little over tarted up — but that's how the public likes its pictures dished up. The R.A. would be in Carey Street in a year if they spent money like that. It will be interesting to see how our public reacts to this exhibition. . . . I am nursing a cold and keeping indoors though I feel quite fit, but am not allowed out yet.

'With all good wishes, Ever yours — Rush.'

Although Rushbury did not, I understand, want my election, he nevertheless stood by me gallantly when I took up the new responsibility and with the other officers of the Academy worked assiduously for its honour and glory.

In his later years I came to know Augustus John well. The bohemian rebel of the twenties became a grand old man of art in the 1950s and 60s. He developed a warm regard, even affection, for the Royal Academy as an institution and some for its President. The exhibition we gave at Burlington House of the works of Mathew Smith, whom he greatly admired, in 1960 increased his attachment to us and to me especially. He told me that Mathew had said to him one day in passing Burlington House, 'at least my work will never be shown there'. When, however, his name appeared in large letters over the entrance John was amused, delighted and grateful. About this time Augustus was painting an ambitious triptych, the subject being the legend of Saintes-Maries-de-la-Mer and he asked me to go down to Fordingbridge to see it. The sureness of hand and mind of the earlier day was waning and more than ever he scraped, altered and hesitated and I think needed someone to lean on so that I received many letters begging me to visit him at Fryern Court. We would lunch together with Dorelia and then spend most of the afternoon in his studio discussing the composition which he had undertaken to finish and send to the Summer Exhibition. I was charmed by the design which had all the Celtic poetry so characteristic of his figure work. Each time I saw it, it became less and less resolved and was never finished and I do not think it has been seen since he died.

Augustus gave me a drawing he made for one of the panels. The drawing, perhaps the last he ever made, is pasted over and over with dozens of fresh pieces of paper to make modifications and this hesitancy is made more obvious when it is placed against another drawing I have with that sure and swift delineation of his hey-day. He could draw then like Van Dyck.

The drawing was lying scattered among many others in the model's throne in the large studio at the bottom of the long garden. Pinned to the wall opposite the entrance were the three panels still in the cartoon stage. The largest roll of canvas I have ever seen was lying at the foot of the triptych. On it was the charcoal drawing for a painting of Canadian soldiers of the 1914-18 war, commissioned, I think, while he was official War Artist attached to the Canadians in France. He spoke of the interest Lord Beaverbrook had shown in the picture and said he would see if something could be done about its completion. Augustus unrolled a portion of it to disclose his masterly and characteristic drawing of that period. All around the walls were stacked or hanging un-finished paintings and life drawings and the floor as well as every available ledge was littered with cigarette ends and match sticks. He smoked incessantly. To say the place was untidy is as much an understatement as to say it was pleasant to be there with John surrounded by exciting evidence of his unique genius.

John was always courteous — a quality which age enhanced in him and which towards me and Muriel developed into affection. On our visits to Fordingbridge we got great pleasure from seeing Augustus and Dorelia, a Darby and Joan having come to rest in the haven of Fryern Court. Dorelia always wore long voluminous skirts, the kind Augustus drew so many times, and looked, as ever, lovely. Augustus wore a skull cap, a woollen sweater and blue cotton slacks. He became somewhat corpulent, she remained slender. In the garden there were two large studios — some 200 yards separated them — and in the house he had a study full of books, busts, drawings and writing materials; and I must not forget his shove ha'penny board. His bedroom on the ground floor was again full of things such as newspaper cuttings pinned on the wall, rough sketches and photos of lovely women or beautiful places. His studios had an air of carelessness about them. I remember one afternoon going into one of them with my wife found a painting placed before an electric fire to dry, so close that it was hot and almost burning. She gently scolded him! His technique was not always faultless, but his every work had a touch of his genius.

When it was time to take our leave Augustus would hug us and, standing side by side with Dorelia at the tall Georgian windows, would wave us goodbye. My last sight of him is in this manner etched upon my memory.

I'm very sorry we never got that triptych for it would have been a thing of great beauty as the photographs we have in the Academy Library, of the cartoon, promise. On the evidence of the photo and my reports the Abbey Trust offered to buy the central panel for £5,000 and give it for the decoration of Burlington House.

In a letter from Hampshire dated 9th March, 1961, John wrote:

'My dear Charles, I have some bad news for you. After working *harder than ever* I have come to the conclusion that I cannot continue without ruining whatever merit these large pictures may have had, nor can I expect to recover such qualities as have been already lost. I want to ask you to release me from my promise to have these things ready for the coming show while there is still time to replace them. *I cannot work against time.* That is now quite obvious: it will be a disappointment for you I know, and perhaps a disaster for me, but it is imperative that I take my own time over these elaborate compositions which positively demand further un-hurried consideration and uninterrupted work if they are to succeed as I feel sure they may. I will not again make un-necessary promises but will return to the work I love with renewed zest and confidence.

'I have told Mr Hutchinson [the Secretary of the Abbey Trust] that I accept his committee's offer on condition that I continue to do my *utmost* to make the work in question worthy of this trust and generosity. May I also count on a (continuance) of your encouragement and true friendship which has been so great a stimulus and guidance.

'With love and apologies,

'Yours ever,

Augustus.'

I could not do otherwise than accept his reasons and absolved him from his promise; to which he replied,

'My very dear Friend,
'I was in great distress when your wire and then your letter came. They saved (my reason) and I am almost myself again. Tooth is sending a car to fetch me tomorrow (to another exhibition at his gallery) for he doesn't trust me — and with reason.

'Yours ever my friend,
'Augustus.'

When, in 1961, at the age of 83 the great painter died, Humphrey Brooke, Maurice Lambert and I went down to Fordingbridge for the funeral service held in the parish church. Apart from many members of his family there were but a few people there. Two or three young art students had 'footed it', from Southampton, I think it was, to pay homage, but the art world in general would seem to have forgotten, not even the Slade was represented. John was buried in Fordingbridge cemetery which was little more than a rough field. As we stood round the grave, the aged Dorelia leaned on the arm of Caspar, then First Sea Lord. Her pale, sad face showed whitely in contrast to the black woollen shawl worn over her head, and she looked like one of those young Irish peasants, but now grown old, in that huge painting *Galway* which at one time had an honoured place in the Tate Gallery — and will again some day. Also on the walls at Millbank, will hang again the painted young Dorelia — *The Smiling Woman*. And the world will pay fresh homage to this Welsh genius.

I am not a clubable man, but I cannot close this chapter without some acknowledgement of the friendships I have made in the Chelsea Arts Club. For over forty years I have been a member and a one-time Chairman. The club house is a small, charming and companionable place — a low, cream-painted, stucco, early Victorian house in Old Church Street with a large garden behind. When I joined as a new member I was very impressed and not a little scared by the men of fame and talent all around. In those days membership consisted of practising artists, sculptors, painters and architects only, which made it a place separate and distinct. Since the war economic pressures have changed that and this unique quality has departed.

Wilson Steer's large, slow moving frame would be seen there each evening playing chess, having first of all hermetically sealed the room by shutting all the windows and doors. The compelling stature of Welsh Augustus John and the small physique of Irish William Orpen would, after dinner, ornament the billiard room where Alexander Fleming, the Scot and discoverer of penicillin (one of the very few honorary members) would be playing snooker before dinner on most evenings when on his way home to Paultons Square from St Mary's Hospital. John Singer Sargent, the American born R.A., George Henry, the Glaswegian, and Thomas Dugdale, the Mancunian, all portrait painters, would boast succession to James McNeill Whistler, one of the earliest painters of the Club. Derwent Wood and Henry Poole would recall memories of Stirling Lee and how the fierce controversy over his nude sculpture on St George's Hall, Liverpool, nearly killed him.

Captain Adrian Jones, the sculptor who lived next door, came in frequently with his navy blue campaign cloak, scarlet lined, flung over his shoulders. (We gave him a party on his 90th birthday.) That great cartoonist of the first war, Australian Will Dyson, etcher and draughtsman and latterly, Academy Keeper, Henry Rushbury and painter David Jagger were buddies together and made a triple centre for dinner-table conviviality. Munnings would walk there for breakfast and always added colour to table talk as well as to the English language — on one occasion so scarlet that he was asked to resign.

During the war the club was a gathering point for those left out of hostilities and of retreat for the members on leave. There was always a hot meal to be had, even when it had to be cooked over a tiny gas flame after bombs had cut the electric power. The steward in those years was one Banks, commonly called 'Pop' who without fail and, except for his wife, singlehanded, kept the club going and helped to look after members' small ailments, minor financial embarrassments and always, the inner man. With members under the table for shelter during raids Pop would go about the business of the place apparently unconcerned. If Pop was a stalwart servant, sculptor Bevan was a stalwart member and Trustee to whom the Club then, before and since, has owed so much.

As I have already said, the war changed the face of club affairs, but it is still a club of character where I have found many friends. It being within walking distance of my studio I frequently go there for lunch and habitually form one of a small band at the end of the long table of scrubbed oak. For half a century I have enjoyed the friendship of William McMillan and worked in the greatest harmony with him on our joint project of the fountains in Trafalgar Square. He is often there for lunch and so is Sir Edward Maufe, the tall, elegant and kindly architect of the beautiful Guildford Cathedral, with whom McMillan and I have worked on several of the War Graves Commission memorials. Vincent Harris, the classical architect, who has built many Town Halls and that splendid circular library at Manchester, helps us to put the modern world into its proper place. Sir Arthur Richmond, son of the distinguished academician, W. B. Richmond, and grandson of academician George Richmond, frequently joins the group and our gay mid-day meal is of simple, honest food, stimulating conversation and good fellowship. Things eagerly to be sought on life's Bill of Fare.

When we have taken our holidays out of England Muriel and I have found great friendliness in the company of Robert Swan, the portrait painter, and Kathleen his wife. Liking the same sort of things we have together sought out places of architectural beauty, Art Galleries, Churches and the lovely countryside, discovering works of art we had not known before. How often have we revelled in Spanish Baroque at Burgos, Salamanca and Toledo and in the Moorish monuments in Granada. Then in that greatest land for

the Arts, Italy, what delights we have enjoyed together in seeing
the glories of the Renaissance, the Romanesque and Gothic periods
in Verona, Florence, Venice and the rest.

There was that never-to-be-forgotten day when studying Piero
Della Francesca in Arezzo we made for Borgo San Sepolcro to
see his famous *Resurrection*. Our Italian driver persuaded us to
make a detour to pass through Monterchi so that we might see
another of the Master's works — who but an Italian chauffeur
would have done this. Following his directions we called at a
caretaker's cottage and were led to the cemetery chapel. When the
door was flung open facing the hill village and the sun at its zenith
we saw Piero's pregnant Madonna of alarming beauty. It provided
one of those highlights in a life's experience which come rarely.
Another came to us on another visit we made to Raphael's birthplace, Urbino. We had heard of frescoes we ought to see, but
which were not listed in the Guide Books. Again, finding the
janitor, we entered the Oratorio de San Giovanni and were
dumbfounded at the glory of the painted walls. Every inch
covered with paintings of the life of the Baptist by the Salambeni
brothers, and all of the highest quality especially the *Crucifixion* on
the east wall. I could go on telling of the virtues of this friendship,
but I must stop for there is more to tell of other things.

CHAPTER ELEVEN

BRONZE AND STONE

SCULPTING WITH CLAY by building up, and then with stone by cutting down I have found absorbing and have done both in about equal amounts and with like zest. The first large work in bronze which attained for me some prominence was a statue of *Spring*. It was difficult to execute because it stood tip-toe on each foot, was highly finished and engraved with spring flowers. This statue was done without a model, but with the knowledge gained from the making of innumerable drawings from life. It was bought for the Chantrey Collection and now occupies, I believe, a place in the basement of the Tate along with Havard Thomas's *Lycidas*, Thornycroft's *Teucer* and works by Mestrovic and Rodin, Reynolds-Stephens and Alfred Stevens, etcetera.

This was followed by an *Aphrodite* which I carved in stone which was also bought for the Chantrey Collection and is likewise sleeping in the cellars. A change over to bronze again and I made a life-sized statue of Adam. Then there is work on buildings, stone statues at the Bank, stone tigers on India House and a gilt bronze springbok on South Africa House: the Madonna and Child for Winchester College and a bronze Guardian Angel over the baptistry of Bishop Jacob Memorial Church at Ilford: many statues in stone and doors in bronze at the Bank: after the war, *Water* and *Earth* carved on Government Offices in Whitehall each from forty tons of Portland stone and bronze groups on the Jellicoe memorial fountain in Trafalgar Square: much stone sculpture and many bronze sculptures on Barclay's Bank head office in Lombard Street, and an 'England Electric' house in the Strand: and so on. The changing mediums of bronze and stone have provided labour for my hands, occupation for my mind, stimulation for my spirit and food, clothing and shelter for me and my family. Through all the labour, as I have indicated, I have been content with my lot.

What artist would not be happy with so many of his works wanted that he has always had some new problems to solve; when he has seen grow from nothing forms which have some meaning for himself and, he hopes, some beauty for others; when he has had no time to get bored, but has found each day challenging and exciting. Where is the sculptor who is not thrilled to stand before a new block of stone with chisel in his left hand and hammer in his right, or who does not go to the bronze foundry with trembling excitement to see his statues cast. And where is he who does not stand at last before his finished work while his spirit aches and his heart sobs in disappointment.

Unless one has experienced the process it is impossible to convey the pleasure a sculptor gets from the practice of his craft. From the moment a new work is commenced he nurses the thought, amounting at times to belief, that this particular creation will be his masterpiece. During the period of gestation, weeks, months or even years in duration, there seem to be infinite possibilities to make it so. But then the day arrives when the labour is completed and the thing he has made is found to be finite and imperfect. How often does a sculptor at this point sink into an abyss from which however he must be rescued through a Promethian hope of one day stealing the fire of Zeus to give life to his clay. 'When the labour is completed', I have said and am reminded that very often have I thought there should be more than one verb for 'to labour' or for 'to work'. How can one equate, for instance, the work of a coal-miner and the work of a sculptor or that of a chimney-sweeper with that of a painter? But since there is only one verb shouldn't artists as well as trades unionists bear the honoured name of 'workers'? It is by labour, though of a vastly different complexion, that we all win a livelihood. And there again there should be several verbs for 'to win', not one. One wins an honest wage, but to 'win' a Football Pool of £300,000 has scarcely the same merit in it. But I am off the point.

When a sculptor carves large blocks of stone, wood or marble, he usually has the assistance of carvers who rough-out and when he models in clay or wax of large size he usually employs casters in plaster and founders in bronze. I have had efficient help throughout my career and been glad of these craftsmen's skill. There are several bronze foundries working still, but very few plaster casters because most modern sculptors build up directly in plaster and need only the help of founders in bronze.

Apart from Chadwick who did much of my plaster casting, I had the help of a craftsman *par excellence* in Charlie Smith, who did work for other sculptors and was always in great demand. Smith was one of those men whom one is genuinely proud to meet. He lived for his work and executed it excellently well and with jealous pride. He was a big man, slow of gait and with a high-pitched voice. Though he cared little for money, he made a lot of it, but spent it hardly. It was a heartening sight to find him coming into the studio carrying a large white enamelled bowl (for mixing Plaster of Paris), a roll of scrim (for reinforcing the plaster) and a collection of odd lengths of iron rods (for bracing the moulds). A long loaf of bread would be protruding from one of his jacket pockets while in another would be a couple of Spanish onions. He would have come to Chelsea, with all this paraphernalia, on a bus from Camden Town. The edibles were for his lunch. His appearance was a welcome sight because one knew his arrival meant that the weeks and months one had spent on making a clay model would result in a perfect reproduction in plaster through Smith's able hands. His overalls were stiff and heavy with plaster splashings and were never cleaned and his boots never scraped after a day's paddling about in gypsum. The soles just wore clean on Chelsea and St John's Wood pavements and one could follow his footsteps far along the road till a bus stop was reached. But what a worker he was, and what skill he had acquired in a long life and in the service of many of the leading sculptors of the day. Such craftsmanship as his is of the salt of the earth.

He would take lunch sitting on a box spread over with newspaper among the debris of plaster chippings. His drink was tea made in the bowl he used to mix his plaster in and the onions he would declare kept him fit. Twenty minutes to half-an-hour was all he would give himself for this repast; then, the short break ended, he would continue working often late into the evening.

When he died I thought he should have an obituary in *The Times*. So I wrote one and it was published in this famous journal which recently refused an obituary of a peeress by a Sitwell because the Editor didn't think she was of sufficient importance. Smith used to say he wanted to die with a bowl of plaster in his hands, and he almost did.

Charles Johnson was a craftsman who helped me with the carving of stone. He was powerful and somewhat crude, but I always finished the carvings myself. He had huge hands and scorned to use a hammer of under four pounds. When he went to Neuve Chapelle to rough-out the tigers I made for the Indian Memorial there, he would beg me to take with me when I went out periodically, supplies of a certain brand of snuff. He would take this throughout his working hours and without it he declared he could not work. Jerry Guidici was another carver who helped me considerably with many carvings including the huge statues of *Earth* and *Water* in Whitehall. Many other assistants have contributed much to my finished sculptures, and to them all I am very grateful.

Willie Wilkinson was one of them. He and I were students together at South Kensington and he came to help me while I was working on the Bank of England sculptures and stayed with me till the war came. Since then he has been fully engaged in film work. Wilkie, like Chadwick, became a friend of the family and would stand on his head and cut funny capers round the studio in order to amuse my children.

When I first began I could not afford help and did all the plaster casting, clay modelling and carving unaided. I had already carved direct the Madonna for Winchester College War Memorial Cloisters without any help, and proceeded to set up, again unaided, the armature and clay model for the large tigers for the Indian Memorial to the Missing on the battlefields of France. Muriel helped me handle tons of clay for this. Afterwards I could afford help and had it in abundance, but I think I was happiest working alone.

When I made the bronze statue of *Adam* I used a young model named Assuati, who had the most perfect male figure have ever seen. He was equally developed all over and not over-muscular anywhere. One often had models with perhaps a small pectoral muscle and a large calf muscle, a developed torso and thin legs, or some such imbalance, but Assuati was perfect in the Polyclitan sense. He used to bring his mandoline and play during rests (the guitar had not then become the rage among teenagers). He fell in love with Muriel's 'mother's help', took her away and married her. The statue was bought for my home town and is now in the Wolverhampton Gallery and so is the limewood 'Mother and Child' I have spoken of.

I could not obtain a model for my next work, which was a gilt bronze springbok for the south-west corner of South Africa House in Trafalgar Square. The Zoo said it would not be possible to keep one in Regent's Park because their leap is so great that in a few hops it would arrive in Baker Street. Drawings of details of similar deer tribes and photographs of them in their natural habitat was all the information I could get. But it was fun making it, though difficult, because of the excessive delicacy and length of the hind legs. I used plasticine for this model. It is a convenient material for certain designs. The wings were added to complete the design and to suggest speed of movement. The gold leaf was laid by a skilled Japanese gilder. My last work has been gilded, where necessary (on the Malta eagle, for instance) by James Butchard who excels the Japanese and who has for many years been making Westminster Abbey splendid with gold. It was a great pleasure and privilege to be able to attend a small party in the Jerusalem Chamber, given by Dean Abbott as a tribute to his many years of skilful gilding of bosses, choir stalls, tombs, etc. in the Abbey.

If Assuati was a most excellent male model, for a female model both my wife and I depended largely on Rachel Fuller. She came to us as a child of fourteen, very shy, slim and lovely and for many years sat for us for sculpture, drawings and paintings. She had a natural aptitude for sitting and could keep a pose for long stretches. Rae sat for many of my works including the Jellicoe fountain and the gilt bronze Ariel on the Bank of England. I made numerous drawings from her and so did many painters. James Gunn painted arms and hands of many of his portraits, including the State Portrait of the Queen, helped by sittings from Rae and Russell Flint and W. E. Webster made her into romantic subject pictures.

For 13 years from the early 1920s, I was making sculpture for the Bank of England then being rebuilt. Baker wanted six large telemones to 'carry up' the line of the John Soane columns to the portico with its pedimental figure of *The Old Lady of Threadneedle Street*. I suggested as a subject *The Bearers and Guardians of Wealth*. They were carved together with the 'Old Lady' *in situ*. My chief concern was to 'marry' my art with the architect's, in which I did not altogether succeed. It was suggested by *The Times* art critic that the sculpture was 'of the day' and the architecture out of date, which, if that were so, was due to the collaboration of men belonging to two generations. Much as Baker and I tried to harmonise there was often a subtle age tension to overcome.

The technical difficulties in making the five pairs of bronze doors surrounding the Bank of England were new and considerable. As I have already said, I was commissioned to execute these at the time my new studio in Tregunter Road was being planned. They were each to be 20 feet high, higher than the dimensions on

57. Adam and Eve: terracotta.

58. Bronze lion group at Invercargill, New Zealand.

59. Sea lion group:
Invercargill.

60. William Walker memorial,
Winchester Cathedral.

61. Her Majesty the Queen:
marble, Royal Academy.

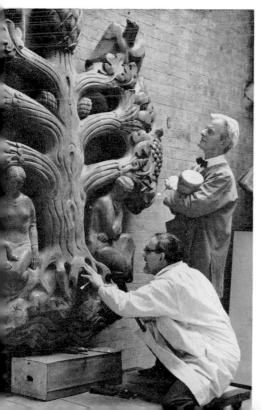

62. Tree of life: teak for the
Carpenters Hall.

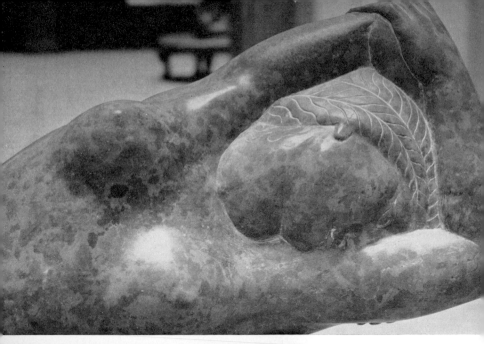

63. Aphrodite III, detail; magnesium limestone, Greenock.

LISTER

THIS TABLET COMMEMORATES
THE CENTENARY CELEBRATIONS
HELD AT THIS COLLEGE TO MARK
LD LISTER'S FIRST PUBLICATION
IN MARCH — APRIL 1867
OF THE ANTISEPTIC
PRINCIPLE IN
SURGERY

64. Lord Lister: marble at the Royal College of Surgeons.

the architect's drawing board at the time. An alteration had therefore to be made to accommodate the new job. Scaffolding and ladders were hired and mounting them day after day carrying heavy clay and plaster was no small physical undertaking; but I was young and fit. When after weeks of modelling the work was ready for moulding new problems had to be faced. Absolute flatness was, of course, essential if the finished doors were to open and shut without difficulty. All warping had to be avoided and much thought went into the problem. We found the answer.

I used often to recall with Chadwick how late one night the mould of the Threadneedle Street doors was at last completed. The last bracing had been added and the final bowl of plaster mixed and hauled up to the top staging where the plaster-caster was working, when it caught a scaffold bar and rained down on to the unfortunate head of one of the helpers. His mop of hair had to be plunged under a running tap because the plaster was rapidly hardening and if it had 'set' would have made the shaving of his head necessary.

After that contretemps the last exciting lowering was begun and I was beset with apprehension for it was a dangerous and delicate operation; but what with sweating, heaving of ropes and swearing, the task was completed at midnight and the mould set safely on the floor ready for the final cast to be taken and, to my utter relief, was found to be straight and true. The warping avoided, the moulders and assistants went home and I to bed very tired but well satisfied with the day's work.

When not modelling in the studio I was carving on the scaffolding in the open air. To be contributing something to the stones of London was to me an ideal occupation, for I have always preferred to have my work placed on buildings rather than on pedestals in museums. In a sense it seems to 'live' more there. Very often did I eat my sandwich lunch sitting on the apex of the pediment over Threadneedle Street watching the life of the city go on below. And once, unlike a working sculptor, I took a rolled umbrella with me up the ladder. It slipped out of my hand, clanked down from floor to floor and landed at the feet of a policeman who, luckily, was holding up the traffic at the time. A small crowd gathered to see, I suppose, if this was a prelude to a suicidal leap by its owner. Should I funk it or should I scramble down and face the music? I did the latter and the kind officer of the law (London policemen are so wonderful) let me pick it up and rush down to hide myself in the subways of the Bank Underground Station. Much relieved, I took the train back to Chelsea and spent the rest of the day far away from the centre of the City.

CHAPTER TWELVE

CONCLUSION

*With some observations on the
present state of the art world*

BY THE VERY NATURE of his work a sculptor is almost literally chained to a stone — the Promethean punishment for trying to give life to his clay. I have never irked at the restraint. It had not been my good fortune therefore to wander from my tetherings further than to Greece to see the marble flowering of Hellenic civilisation. But many revolutions have occurred in my life time, and whereas in my youth a magic carpet would have to have been conjured up to travel rapidly over the face of the earth, it is now possible through the marvellously speedy development of the aeroplane for you and me to reach the Antipodes in 36 hours.

When invited to go to New Zealand to discuss a large sculptural project, it was possible for me to leave the work on hand in the studio for 30 days and circumnavigate the globe.

In the very harsh winter of 1963 I left the snow covered Surrey hills on a morning late in February and set out on what was for me a fantastic exploration. It must be remembered that I was then three score years and ten and it might be expected that my first adventure into the element of air — which until I grew up, remained aloof from man but which, in the twentieth century he has probed with audacious familiarity — would not be taken without some misgivings. And so it was. However, they were very soon overcome and I found the new form of travel exhilarating and without fears. It was not so much the new cloudscapes as the clear brightness of the sun forever shining that acted like a tonic on my spirits. I had never seen Phoebus so lightly clad and I would fly everywhere if I could reach above the clouds.

In New York I was met by sculptor Bryant Baker, who had been a student at the Royal Academy Schools and who, going early in life to the States, has made a considerable reputation with his marble statues and busts. He took me to a meeting of the National Academy of Design where I was presented with their gold medal. I reciprocated with one from the Royal Academy.

In Central Park I was able to study the three groups of sculpture — *Alice in Wonderland*, *Hans Anderson* and *Mother Goose* — placed there for the pleasure of New York children. I thought them far too pictorial, but there was no doubt about the enjoyment the children got from them and the bronze was highly polished where it had been handled and sat upon. My sculptures for New Zealand were for a similar purpose, but I decided they should not be sentimentalised as these were. If the pants of juvenile Invercargillians would polish my bronzes that would add a lovely patina to what other merit they might possess, and that would be gain for me and fun for them. I always wanted to see some of my sculpture not on pedestals or high on buildings but close to the ground as is the bronze boar in the market place in Florence, on which the Florentine boys and girls climb and give to it a metallic surface of great beauty. Now I was to have my chance.

While in the great city I met my brother Victor whom I had not seen for 30 years. He came from Washington to join me. Together we did the sights including the ugly United Nations building. I found it hopelessly depressing. The one ray of pleasure came from seeing a bronze replica of the Greek *Thundering Zeus*, the original of which I had seen in the National Museum in Athens a few months after it had been salved from the sea bed where it had lain for over two thousand years, and had acquired a most marvellous green patina. The copy was a gift from the Greek Government. The work of art apart from this, which gave me the greatest thrill was the self-portrait of Rembrandt in the Frick Museum. It overpowered me with its force and pathos. This and the tremendous picture *Polish Rider* would justify any pilgrimage from anywhere in the world to the Frick.

There were queues half a mile long to see Gioconda in the Metropolitan. Coach loads waited 'To spend a half day with Mona Lisa and have tea'. (Advert.) and there were crowds to see Rembrandt's *Plato contemplating the bust of Homer* which had just been acquired for a record sum. Then there was a comprehensive Kandinsky exhibition in the new Gugenheim museum, that silly building by Frank Lloyd Wright, and so New York was buzzing with 'culture'. As P.R.A. I was received by Directors Lorimer of the Metropolitan, Arnason of the Gugenheim and Biekel of the Frick with great courtesy. Indeed, wherever I went on this trip round the world, because of my office, I was honoured. The Prime Minister of New Zealand, Mr Holyoake, in his room in Government Buildings, welcomed me in the name of his country. I was very proud to find my Academy so well thought of in far away places.

Not alone did the bad U.N. building depress me, but an ugliness of a different sort is referred to in my diary from which I quote: 'Everyone I have met has been kind and courteous, but one horror will remain for ever in my mind and that is Wall Street and the Stock Exchange. . . . The milling crowds of brokers, clerks and messengers, their pale and eager faces, their pencils and tablets, their discarded chits littering the ground ankle deep on which they stood, the running tapes at each corner, the flickering check-boards, the crushing crowded mercenary booths scattered over the whole area of ant-hill like activity made me sick at heart and long to be back painting the English landscape.'

My stay at Hawaii was made pleasant and memorable by the kindness of Terry and Ria Parker, the charming friends of the New Zealand High Commissioner in London — Sir Thomas Macdonald. I had not met them before, but they greeted me like an old friend and were kindness itself. The Honolulu Academy of Arts is a good simple building of one storey, built round several open courts. I was surprised to see so many fine paintings and sculptures there. They included carvings from India, China and

Japan and some masterpieces of Chinese painting including *The Goose Frieze* which was such a feature of the Chinese Exhibition in the Royal Academy in 1935–36. The collection included one of the finest Gauguins I have seen.

After breakfasting under the same banyan tree whose branches once spread over the bent head and writing tablets of Robert Louis Stevenson, the aeroplane took me to Fiji. I was impressed by the beauty of this island and thought if I could build an Earthly Paradise I should start it there.

I was taken to see a native Fijian village. The houses of wooden frames were thatched and had walls of plaited rushes, were simple in design and picturesquely placed beneath bread-fruit and umbrella trees, papaya and coconut pines. Their Chief or 'queen' as she is now called, welcomed us to her large dwelling similar in style to the cottages, but, of course, far grander and made for her by her tribesmen working continuously for four months by sun and moon. She told me she ruled over three thousand, four hundred Fijians. While we were chatting a serving girl dressed in rose pink squatted in a dark corner, grinning and showing excessively white teeth from out the gloom. A large coloured photograph of Queen Elizabeth and Prince Philip was prominently displayed on a central table. It was a recent gift from Her Majesty.

When I arrived at Auckland from Fiji I was met by an old colleague sculptor John Kavanagh, whom I had not seen since he emigrated to teach in Auckland many years ago. Although I was to some extent instrumental in his appointment there I regretted his leaving England because I very much admired his art. Had he stayed here I think he would have been one of the leading sculptors of the day.

Many of the places of great natural beauty were shown to me both in the North and South Islands. Places like Rotorua, Milford Sound and Queenstown, but it was the town nearest to the South Pole which was the place I had really come to visit and the purpose of the visit was to discuss an unusual sculptural scheme with the Mayor of Invercargill. A well-known citizen had not long died leaving a bequest for sculpture to be placed in Queen's Park there 'for the enjoyment of children' and I had been invited to make it The conditions appealed to me and so I had come some twelve thousand miles with a maquette to show to members of the Town Council of the design I had made. Among the benefactor's townsmen I met one of his particular friends who described J. B. Thomson as 'a bachelor who had an inordinate love of children'. He would fill his pockets with coins and take his afternoon stroll round the town distributing largesse to young Invercargillians so that they could buy sweets or go to the cinema or purchase some other thing they wanted. On one of these walks my informant was with him when J.B.T. looked at his watch and found it was time to keep an appointment, so he emptied the contents of his pockets into his friend's hands with the injunction 'Carry on the good work'.

Neil Watson, the Mayor, his Councillors, prominent citizens and I all got on well together, the commission was signed and sealed and for the following three years I laboured to make a fountain surmounted by The Infant Pan, and groups of bronze animals placed low on the ground and designed so that children could climb up, ride on their backs and generally take that delight which is natural to children, in the animal world. Queen Elizabeth, the Queen Mother, unveiled these bronzes in Queen's Park when she visited the Antipodes.

This long and ridiculously brief journey ended, its purpose fulfilled. I was obliged to hurriedly return to preside at the Academy over the arrangements for the Summer Exhibition and to continue with the many sculptures which, half finished, awaited completion in my studio. As well as these I now had to commence work on the large bronzes just planned.

As I write these closing sentences of the short story telling of a life's journeying, I have reached another important milestone. For I have handed over the reins at the Academy to another President, Tom Monnington. He will be faced with situations as difficult of solution as those with which I had to wrestle during my time. It

would be unnatural in me if I were not troubled and anxious
about the future of our historic Institution as it prepares to reach a
milestone on which is inscribed '200 years' and it would be gross
of me not to hope that my successor will succeed better than I have
done, with problems palpable and impalpable concerning the
Royal Academy. It was a tremendous honour for me to wear for
so long the mantle of Sir Joshua Reynolds; and now that I have
shed it regrets will be numerous but compensations lavish, for I
shall be able to wear more often my studio working clothes which
are no less honourable, more comfortable and a little warmer
round the heart.

On concluding these pages I am able to look back on more than
half a century during which good fortune has kept me company.
If my career had been left to the mercy of my abilities alone, if I
had not had a good constitution — if I had not met Muriel —
Baker — Emerson and many other inspirers and helpers, how
different would have been my story. If I had been born a hundred
years earlier or later how otherwise would have run my tale.

But this century has produced a glut of eventful things which
have given it form and colour to paint a disturbed and disturbing
image of our times. Politically, socially, militarily, technologically,
scientifically, culturally and so on, enormous changes have taken
place. The arts have been busy following their traditional role of
reflecting the period in which they were made.

There have been violent changes in the outlook of my contem-
poraries, not all fellow travellers. Some time ago I took the
trouble to count up the number of 'isms' which had gained
currency during the preceding 40 years. I was able to name 30,
most of them already gone into the limbo of forgotten things.
I have witnessed the breaking of many artistic faiths and the
jettisoning of many art-disciplines. The greatest of these faiths was
a belief in objective values. This has gone. The greatest of the
discards that of drawing. Whereas Ingres' dictum was 'The
probity of art is drawing', the present assertion would seem to be
'The probity of art is colour'. Colour is a lesser discipline.

These two factors have altered the face of art considerably. If you uproot one faith you must plant another. Objective values having been discounted, belief in the ego and subjective values has been taken up. The ego has been set on a very high pedestal. Subjective values are of course of great importance, but I believe they should operate in a framework of positive controls. When you dispense with discipline you push the fences down and in rush the labour-savers, opportunists and charlatans. Since the ending of the last war interest in the Fine Arts has greatly increased. This has led to a multiplication of art dealers. They must have quintupled in London in twenty years. Now art dealers have to find pictures to sell and pictures cannot be supplied to them quickly enough or in sufficient numbers if the same attention has to be given to their craft and drawing as was given by — shall we say — Jan Van Eyck. Any 'Van Eyck' then of today is 'out'. A whole year or more might be taken to produce one Van Eyck. This is not good enough.

Modern art dealers must have 30 or more works of art for an exhibition lasting a month or so and it is not infrequently that one reads of a young man having his third one man show before he is 30. Therefore art dealers encourage that form of art which discards drawing and good craftsmanship as requisites. After all Van Eyck made pictures to endure, but since that brilliant American invention 'planned obsolescence' has been such a commercial success why should not works of art also bow the knee. This, it would seem, is the plan. I do not refer, of course, to the great houses such as Agnews and Colnaghis.

The present day art dealing industry has been built up on the new faith in the ego as well as on the lack of the love of discipline. Many painters and sculptors being dwarfs are put upon the stage in giant's boots; and zany clowns, it is claimed, utter prophesies. It has been said elsewhere that there are so many great artists, but so few good painters. The ego is blown up by the blurb in the normal art dealer's catalogue which, with incomprehensible verbosity behind a cloak of profound-seeming obscurantism, conceals weaknesses, confuses and misguides. It has become increasingly the practice to start previews with glasses of sherry or champagne — why? A good picture needs no wine as good wine needs no bush. However, good business, I suppose, does.

Alas it is that any new kink or gimmick captures more attention than does merit and sensation is preferred to excellence. (While I am writing this I hear of an 'artist' who throws boxes under buses and then they are exhibited as artistic creations.) Is there no limit to these stunts. All this is a malaise which feeds on words, words which have got out of hand. It is my belief that if a law could be passed forbidding art criticism for ten years it would be found that painting and sculpture had returned to health having in the meantime been nourished by *looking* at form, colour and light and shade without the accompaniment of so much confusing and misleading terminology.

I will quote one example taken recently from an American University Journal: 'The artist has to accept self-destruction in order to be able to create. I myself believe that creativeness does not so much sublimate libidinous urges as it serves to absorb self-destructive Thanatos urges. The relief which comes with the rhythmical disintegration and re-integration of ego functions during creative activity may be connected with the absorption and neutralization of self-destructive Thanatos urges which otherwise would destroy the ego. The psychotic's overwhelming dread of self-destruction prevents the free oscillation of this rhythm and thereby eliminates the only remedy which could restore his disintegrated personality.' Many painters, no doubt, have experienced this relief and have congratulated themselves on the narrow escape of their ego from disintegration. What would Turner have thought of this, I wonder; what Velasquez?

I fear that most modern art critics are of a low standard. Only Sir Kenneth Clark can compare with John Ruskin, both of whom were better called 'art historians'. We think today that everything can be explained by writing and talking. Everything cannot. Much of art is in this category. The words 'contemporary', 'advanced', 'experimental' are some of the adjectives which are regarded as sacrosanct and are to be questioned at peril of one's being ostracised by very 'U' society. They are written large over the portal of the Tate Gallery and on the bunting flown from its flagstaff. Under the Directorship of Sir John Rothenstein, many monstrous, cumbersome and incompetent works have been shown in the galleries of Millbank. Mr Norman Reid is now busy gilding the lettering. Crazy creations are produced and defended by the wielding of these wordy weapons and not only in this one time 'National Gallery of British Art', but in galleries and museums, private and public in other places in this country and the world. A pernicious form of art-snobbery has taken hold of us, and has effectively silenced even otherwise sensible souls into submission. Our art-coin is debased.

As I have gone about as P.R.A. over wide fields and into many camps I have been astonished at the common bewilderment prevailing among men and women everywhere. They have often said to me: 'Tell me, should I like such and such a picture' or 'ought I to admire the sculpture of Mr So-and-So because the art critic of the *Daily Paper* says they are works of great significance'; or they will tell me the Tate, or the Metropolitan or the Guggenheim has bought one of Mr X's works — as though that were the ultimate! Few of us relish being out of the swim, but fashions prevail for a short while only and then fortunately fade away. When the current ones have gone what, I wonder, will take their place?

Art dealing has now come to the front as a world industry. The Venice Biennale provides an international market-place where reputations are built up and exchanged. Whether this is good for the Arts is, I think, very doubtful. Indeed my personal conviction is that it is harmful for the reasons I have given. It has led too often to blatant showmanship and to insincerity as well as to an irresponsible traffic in works of art unparalleled in the great days of true genius and the perspicacious private patron. But these are not great days of the arts, or so I fear, nor of cultivated patronage for all the official backing painters and sculptors now get. (When the Postmaster General uses the design for a postage stamp by a mere infant at the same time as the Minister of Education is spending thousands of pounds on training art students to be competent for such a job, we are given an example of the 'enlightenment' of governmental patronage.) No. The Fine Arts are at a low ebb as truly as the sciences are in full flood. Who will mint us a new art coin of sterling worth? On the obverse might be struck, for inspiration, the head of Michelangelo and on the reverse for guidance the one word 'Beauty'.

I cannot let go the conviction that there will be one day, that indeed there *must* be a Renaissance. (The art world is now too crackpot to endure for long.) The day of its coming would be hastened if only influential laymen, not artists like me, would say frankly what they think. But they won't because they are too timid. Several of them have admitted it to me. One of the most important of them said when challenged: 'But I have to be so careful you know.'

Since I am free of my Presidential responsibilities and speak now for myself alone I can tell of my beliefs with uninhibited candour.

I wish my final words to be of the Royal Academy to which I have rendered some service. Since I have fought for its health and independence it would be unnatural of me were I now to be careless of its destiny. In the nature of things institutions may grow ancient but they need not grow old in spirit.

The two chief problems the Academy has to wrestle with are, first, how to keep a sane attitude to the changing conditions of the times and, second, how to avoid the incursion of outside interference. The former is the more urgent and the latter not to be under-rated.

While I have witnessed admirable things at Burlington House I have seen a few foolish ones too. The first problem has been handled dangerously by some members who have too often flirted with the critics and have sometimes hung the Summer Exhibition with too much thought for them. To think of pleasing the Press is to court disaster and therefore I hope this attitude will be done away with. I know it has a double intention — to make the exhibition 'a success' by the hoped-for consequent favourable newspaper reviews, and to make it seem that we are up with the *avant garde*. This is not the way to avoid hardening of the Academy's arteries. The way for us to avoid growing old is for our members to look inwards to the honest conviction of their heart and mind. Then and then alone will each successive generation of A.R.A.s and R.A.s keep the spirit of their heritage vigorous and young. We must beware of the dangers associated with cliques and remember the vital importance of the individualistic outlook, inherent upon the separate and peculiar contribution that each can make to the health of the whole. Therefore the Academy must dismiss as quite impossible any take over bid if ever it is made. It must persist in paying its own way as it has always done and if the time comes to a successor, as it came to me, when financial difficulties threaten to overwhelm him, I believe he will not fear to sell the great Michelangelo Tondo even though that were as painful to him and his colleagues as the selling of the Leonardo Cartoon was to me and mine.

INDEX

INDEX

INDEX